POE'S SHORT STORIES

Edgar Allan Poe

EDITORIAL DIRECTOR Justin Kestler
EXECUTIVE EDITOR Ben Florman

SERIES EDITORS Boomie Aglietti, John Crowther, Justin Kestler
PRODUCTION Christian Lorentzen

WRITER Matthew Benedetto
EDITORS Boomie Aglietti, Benjamin Morgan

This edition published by Spark Publishing

Spark Publishing
A Division of SparkNotes LLC
120 Fifth Avenue, 8th Floor
New York, NY 10011

02 03 04 05 SN 9 8 7 6 5 4 3 2 1

Please send all comments and questions or report errors to
feedback@sparknotes.com.

Library of Congress information available upon request

Printed and bound in the United States

RRD-C

ISBN 1-58663-452-6

Introduction:
Stopping to
Buy Sparknotes
On a
Snowy Evening

Whose words these are you *think* you know.
Your paper's due tomorrow, though;
We're glad to see you stopping here
To get some help before you go.

Lost your course? You'll find it here.
Face tests and essays without fear.
Between the words, good grades at stake:
Get great results throughout the year.

Once school bells caused your heart to quake
As teachers circled each mistake.
Use SparkNotes and no longer weep,
Ace every single test you take.

Yes, books are lovely, dark, and deep,
But only what you grasp you keep,
With hours to go before you sleep,
With hours to go before you sleep.

Contents

Context

EDGAR ALLAN POE WAS BORN on January 19, 1809, and died on October 7, 1849. In his stormy forty years, which included a marriage to his cousin, fights with other writers, and legendary drinking binges, Poe lived in all the important literary centers of the northeastern United States: Baltimore, Philadelphia, New York City, and Boston. He was a magazine editor, a poet, a short story writer, a critic, and a lecturer. He introduced the British horror story, or the Gothic genre, to American literature, along with the detective story, science fiction, and literary criticism. Poe became a key figure in the nineteenth-century flourishing of American letters and literature. Famed twentieth-century literary critic F.O. Matthiessen named this period the American Renaissance. He argued that nineteenth-century American writers Ralph Waldo Emerson, Henry David Thoreau, Nathaniel Hawthorne, Herman Melville, and Walt Whitman crafted a distinctly American literature that attempts to escape from the long shadow of the British literary tradition. Matthiessen paid little attention to Edgar Allan Poe. Although he long had a reputation in Europe as one of America's most original writers, only in the latter half of the twentieth century has Poe been viewed as a crucial contributor to the American Renaissance.

The often tragic circumstances of Poe's life haunt his writings. His father disappeared not long after the child's birth, and, at the age of three, Poe watched his mother die of tuberculosis. Poe then went to live with John and Frances Allan, wealthy theatergoers who knew his parents, both actors, from the Richmond, Virginia, stage. Like Poe's mother, Frances Allan was chronically ill, and Poe experienced her sickness much as he did his mother's. His relationship with John Allan, who was loving but moody, generous but demanding, was emotionally turbulent. With Allan's financial help, Poe attended school in England and then enrolled at the University of Virginia in 1826, but he was forced to leave after two semesters. Although Poe blamed Allan's stinginess, his own gambling debts played a large role in his fiscal woes. A tendency to cast blame on others, without admitting his own faults, characterized Poe's relationship with many people, most significantly Allan. Poe struggled with a view of Allan as a false father, generous enough to take him in at age three, but never dedicated enough to adopt him as a true son. There are echoes of Poe's upbringing in his works, as sick mothers and guilty fathers appear in many of his tales.

After leaving the University of Virginia, Poe spent some time in the military before he used his contacts in Richmond and Baltimore to enter the magazine industry. With little experience, Poe relied on his characteristic bravado to convince Thomas Willis White, then head of the fledgling *Southern Literary Messenger,* to take him on as an editor in 1835. This position gave him a forum for his early tales, including "Berenice" and "Morella." The *Messenger* also established Poe as a leading and controversial literary critic, who often attacked his New England counterparts—especially poet Henry Wadsworth Longfellow—in the genteel pages of the magazine. Poe ultimately fell out of favor with White, but his literary criticism made him a popular speaker on the lecture circuit. Poe never realized his most ambitious dream—the launch of his own magazine, the *Stylus*. Until his death, he believed that the New England literary establishment had stolen his glory and had prevented the *Stylus* from being published.

His name has since become synonymous with macabre tales like "The Tell-Tale Heart," but Poe assumed a variety of literary personas during his career. The *Messenger*—as well as *Burton's Gentleman's Magazine* and *Graham's*—established Poe as one of America's first popular literary critics. He advanced his theories in popular essays, including "The Philosophy of Composition" (1846), "The Rationale of Verse" (1848), and "The Poetic Principle." In "The Philosophy of Composition" Poe explained how he had crafted "The Raven," the 1845 poem that made him nationally famous. In the pages of these magazines, Poe also introduced of a new form of short fiction—the detective story—in tales featuring the Parisian crime solver C. Auguste Dupin. The detective story follows naturally from Poe's interest in puzzles, word games, and secret codes, which he loved to present and decode in the pages of the *Messenger* to dazzle his readers. The word "detective" did not exist in English at the time that Poe was writing, but the genre has become a fundamental mode of twentieth-century literature and film. Dupin and his techniques of psychological inquiry have informed countless sleuths, including Sir Arthur Conan Doyle's Sherlock Holmes and Raymond Chandler's Philip Marlowe.

Gothic literature, a genre that rose with Romanticism in Britain in the late eighteenth century, explores the dark side of human experience—death, alienation, nightmares, ghosts, and haunted land-scapes. Poe brought the Gothic to America. American Gothic literature dramatizes a culture plagued by poverty and slavery through characters afflicted with various forms of insanity and mel-ancholy. Poe, America's foremost southern writer before William Faulkner, generated a Gothic ethos from his own experiences in Vir-ginia and other slaveholding territories, and the black and white imagery in his stories reflects a growing national anxiety over the issue of slavery.

In the spectrum of American literature, the Gothic remains in the shadow of the dominant genre of the American Renaissance—the Romance. Popularized by Nathaniel Hawthorne, Romantic litera-ture, like Gothic literature, relies on haunting and mysterious narra-tives that blur the boundary between the real and the fantastic. Poe's embrace of the Gothic with its graphic violence and disturbing sce-narios places him outside the ultimately conservative and tradi-tional resolutions of Romantic novels such as Hawthorne's *The House of the Seven Gables* (1851).

In Romances like the novels of Hawthorne, conflicts occur among characters within the context of society and are resolved in accordance with society's rules. Poe's Gothic tales are brief flashes of chaos that flare up within lonely narrators living at the fringes of society. Poe's longest work, the 1838 novel *Arthur Gordon Pym,* described in diary form a series of episodes on a journey to Antarc-tica. A series of bizarre incidents and exotic discoveries at sea, *Pym* lacks the cohesive elements of plot or quest that tie together most novels and epics and is widely considered an artistic failure. Poe's style and concerns never found their best expression in longer forms, but his short stories are considered masterpieces worldwide. The Poe's Gothic is a potent brew, best served in small doses.

PLOT OVERVIEW

MS. FOUND IN A BOTTLE (1833)

A voyage in the South Seas is swept off course by a hurricane, and the narrator responds to the life-threatening turn of events.

LIGEIA (1858)

"Ligeia" describes the two marriages of the narrator, the first to the darkly featured and brilliant Lady Ligeia; the second to her racial opposite, the fair and blonde Lady Rowena. Both women die quickly and mysteriously after their marriage ceremonies, and the narrator's persistent memories of Ligeia bring her back to life to replace Lady Rowena's corpse.

THE FALL OF THE HOUSE OF USHER (1939)

A woman also returns from the dead in "The Fall of the House of Usher." The story's narrator is summoned by his boyhood friend Roderick Usher to visit him during a period of emotional distress. The narrator discovers that Roderick's twin sister, Madeline, is also sick. She takes a turn for the worse shortly after the narrator's arrival, and the men bury Madeline in a tomb within the house. They later discover, to their horror, that they have entombed her alive. Madeline claws her way out, collapsing eventually on Roderick, who dies in fear.

WILLIAM WILSON (1839)

Poe again takes up the theme of the twin in "William Wilson." The narrator discovers that a classmate shares not only the name William Wilson but also his physical build, style of dress, and even vocal intonation. A fear of losing of his identity drives the narrator to murder his rival, but the crime also mysteriously brings about his own death.

THE MURDERS IN THE RUE MORGUE (1841)

In this detective story, Poe introduces the brilliant sleuth C. Auguste Dupin. When the Paris police arbitrarily arrest Dupin's friend for the gruesome murders of a mother and daughter, Dupin begins an independent investigation and solves the case accurately. Uncovering evidence that goes otherwise unnoticed, Dupin concludes that a wild animal, an Ourang-Outang, committed the murders.

THE TELL-TALE HEART (1843)

Obsessed with the vulture-like eye of an old man he otherwise loves and trusts, the narrator smothers the old man, dismembers his body, and conceals the parts under the floorboards of the bedroom. When the police arrive to investigate reports of the old man's shrieks, the narrator attempts to keep his cool, but hears what he thinks is the beating of the old man's heart. Panicking, afraid that the police know his secret, he rips up the floorboards and confesses his crime.

THE PIT AND THE PENDULUM (1843)

Captured by the Inquisition, the narrator fends off hungry rats, avoids falling into a giant pit, and escapes the razor-sharp blades of a descending pendulum. As the walls of his cell are about to close in and drive him into the pit, he is saved by the French army.

THE BLACK CAT (1843)

When the narrator hangs a cat he had formerly adored, the cat returns from the dead to haunt him. The narrator tries to strike back at the cat but kills his wife in the process. The cat draws the police to the cellar wall where the narrator has hidden his wife's corpse.

THE PURLOINED LETTER (1844)

In this sequel to "The Murders in the Rue Morgue," Dupin recovers a stolen letter to foil a villain's plan. The police attempt thorough investigations but come up with nothing. Identifying with the criminal mind, Dupin discovers evidence so obvious that it had gone unnoticed.

THE MASQUE OF THE RED DEATH (1845)

A bloody disease called the Red Death ravages a kingdom. Prince Prospero retreats to his castle and throws a lavish masquerade ball to celebrate his escape from death. At midnight, a mysterious guest arrives and, as the embodiment of the Red Death, kills Prospero and all his guests.

THE CASK OF AMONTILLADO (1846)

The vengeful Montresor repays the supposed insults of his enemy, Fortunato. Luring Fortunato into the crypts of his home with the promise of Amontillado sherry, Montresor entombs Fortunato in a wall while the carnival rages above them.

CHARACTER LIST

"MS. FOUND IN A BOTTLE"

Unnamed narrator A world traveler and survivor of two hurricanes at sea. After a mishap on the South Seas, the narrator embarks on a journey of self-discovery to regions beyond human exploration and rational knowledge.

Old Swede Along with the narrator, the only survivor of the tale's first hurricane. The Old Swede's experience of the tragic voyage is purely physical, not intellectual like the narrator's. His death signals the metaphoric importance of the voyage as a quest for knowledge.

"LIGEIA"

Unnamed narrator Husband of both Lady Ligeia and Lady Rowena. Unable to recall certain details about his only love, Ligeia, the narrator keeps her alive in his memory after her physical death and his second marriage.

Ligeia The darkly beautiful and learned first wife of the narrator, Ligeia is a woman who returns from the grave. After dying from a mysterious illness, Ligeia haunts her husband and his new bride, becoming part of the Gothic decorations of their bridal chamber.

Lady Rowena The blonde second wife of the narrator. Rowena's cold English character contrasts with Ligeia's sensual, Germanic romanticism. Ligeia punishes Rowena's lack of affection for the narrator by haunting the bridal chamber and dooming their marriage.

"The Fall of the House of Usher"

Roderick Usher The owner of the mansion and last male in the Usher line. Roderick functions as a doppelganger, or character double, for his twin sister, Madeline. He represents the mind to her body and suffers from the mental counterpart of her physical illness.

Madeline Usher Roderick's twin sister and victim of catalepsy, a mysterious incapacitating illness. Because the narrator is surprised to discover that Madeline is a twin, she signals the narrator's outsider relationship to the house of Usher.

Unnamed narrator Roderick's best boyhood friend. Contacted by Roderick during his emotional distress, the narrator knows little about the house of Usher and is the first outsider to visit the mansion in many years.

"William Wilson"

William Wilson The narrator who murders his double, also named William Wilson. The first William Wilson suffers from a split personality: he takes a figment of his imagination and gives it physical shape.

William Wilson A classmate and rivalrous competitor of the narrator. This second William Wilson is the external embodiment of the narrator's paranoia.

"The Murders in the Rue Morgue"

C. Auguste Dupin A Parisian crime solver. Dupin discovers the truth behind the violent murders of two women after the Paris police arrest the wrong man. He employs psychological analysis and intuition and considers possibilities not imagined by the police to conclude that the murders were committed by an Ourang-Outang.

Madame L'Espanaye The older of the two Parisian murder victims. Violently beaten with a club, Madame L'Espanaye dies from a cut throat and is thrown through the window to a courtyard below her apartment.

Mademoiselle Camille Daughter of Madame L'Espanaye. Mademoiselle Camille is choked to death by the murderer and then stuffed into the chimney.

Adolphe Le Bon A bank clerk and the first suspect in the two murders.

Unnamed narrator A friend and housemate of Dupin. The narrator attempts to provide an objective chronicle of the crime, but his tone celebrates Dupin's brilliance.

Sailor The owner of the Ourang-Outang. The sailor witnesses the two murders but is unable to interfere. His inability to restrain the Ourang-Outang also represents the limits of the Paris police to imagine a nonhuman explanation for the vicious murders.

"THE TELL-TALE HEART"

Unnamed narrator The murderer of the old man. Addressing the reader, the narrator offers his tale of precise murder and dismemberment as an argument for his sanity.

Old man The narrator's murder victim. The narrator's obsession with the old man's one vulture-eye indicates the insanity that the narrator wants to deny.

"THE PIT AND THE PENDULUM"

Unnamed narrator A victim of the Inquisition. The narrator maintains sanity that many of Poe's other narrators lack. He functions with Dupin-like practicality despite the invisible enemy threatening him with torture.

General Lasalle A leader of the French army. General Lasalle is a real and positive presence of authority in contrast to the shadowy and invisible leaders of the Inquisition.

"THE BLACK CAT"

Unnamed narrator The murderer of his wife. Haunted by a favorite cat that he hanged, the narrator seeks revenge, only to lash out against his wife.

Narrator's wife The murder victim. Also a lover of animals, the narrator's wife defends the second cat from her husband's anger. She possesses the generosity that the narrator has mysteriously lost.

"THE PURLOINED LETTER"

C. Auguste Dupin A savvy and learned Parisian who helps the city's police solve crimes. Dupin uses psychology to foil the plans of a thief and uncover a stolen letter that the police of Paris could not uncover by conventional investigations.

Unnamed narrator A friend of Dupin. In awe of Dupin's brilliance, the narrator faithfully recounts Dupin's explanations without doubting or challenging him.

Monsieur G—— The Prefect of the Paris police. Limited by his conventional police training, Monsieur G—— depends on Dupin's assistance in peculiarly difficult crimes, and his own general competence highlights Dupin's superior abilities.

Minister D—— A government official and the thief of the letter. Minister D—— 's ability to outwit the police in his crime proves he is a worthy adversary for Dupin.

"THE MASQUE OF THE RED DEATH"

Prince Prospero A wealthy nobleman and the ultimate victim of the Red Death. Prince Prospero's wealth turns out to be irrelevant in the natural cycle of life and death.

Mysterious guest The embodiment of the Red Death. Donning the gruesome marks of the plague as his costume, the mysterious guest brings death to those who deny their own mortality.

"THE CASK OF AMONTILLADO"

Montresor The narrator, Montresor, murders Fortunato for insulting him by walling him up alive behind bricks in a wine cellar.

Fortunato A wine expert murdered by Montresor. Dressed as a court jester, Fortunato falls prey to Montresor's scheme at a particularly carefree moment during a carnival.

ANALYSIS OF MAJOR CHARACTERS

RODERICK USHER

As one of the two surviving members of the Usher family in "The Fall of the House of Usher," Roderick is one of Poe's character doubles, or doppelgangers. Roderick is intellectual and bookish, and his twin sister, Madeline, is ill and bedridden. Roderick's inability to distinguish fantasy from reality resembles his sister's physical weakness. Poe uses these characters to explore the philosophical mystery of the relationship between mind and body. With these twins, Poe imagines what would happen if the connection between mind and body were severed and assigned to separate people. The twin imagery and the incestuous history of the Usher line establish that Roderick is actually inseparable from his sister. Although mind and body are separated, they remain dependent on each other for survival. This interdependence causes a chain reaction when one of the elements suffers a breakdown. Madeline's physical death coincides with the collapse of both Roderick's sanity and the Ushers' mansion.

C. AUGUSTE DUPIN

In the stories "The Murders in the Rue Morgue" and "The Purloined Letter," Poe creates the genre of detective fiction and the original expert sleuth, C. Auguste Dupin. In both "The Murders in the Rue Morgue" and "The Purloined Letter," Dupin works outside conventional police methods, and he uses his distance from traditional law enforcement to explore new ways of solving crimes. He continually argues that the Paris police exhibit stale and unoriginal methods of analysis. He says that the police are easily distracted by the specific facts of the crime and are unable to provide an objective standpoint from which to investigate. In "The Murders in the Rue Morgue," the police cannot move beyond the gruesome nature of the double homicide. Because they are so distracted by the mutilated and choked victims, they do not closely inspect the windows of the apartment, which reveal a point of entry and escape. Dupin distances himself from the emotional aspect of the scene's violence. Like a mathematician, he views the crime scene as a site of calculation, and he considers the moves of the murderer as though pitted against him in a chess game.

In "The Purloined Letter," Dupin solves the theft of the letter by putting himself at risk politically. Whereas the Paris police tread lightly around the actions of Minister D——, an important government official, Dupin ignores politics just as he ignores emotion in the gruesome murders of the Rue Morgue. In this story, Dupin reveals his capacity for revenge. When the Minister insulted him in Vienna years before the crime presently in question, Dupin promised to repay the slight. This story demonstrates that Dupin's brilliance is not always dispassionately mathematical. He cunningly analyzes the external facts of the crime, but he is also motivated by his hunger for revenge. Dupin must function as an independent detective because his mode of investigation thrives on intuition and personal cunning, which cannot be institutionalized in a traditional police force.

WILLIAM WILSON

Poe explores the imagery of doubles in "William Wilson." William Wilson loses his personal identity when he discovers a classmate who shares not only his full name but also his physical appearance and manner of speaking. Poe stresses the external aspects of their similarity less than the narrator's mental turmoil, which is triggered by his encounter with his rivalrous double. When the narrator attempts to murder his double in the story's final moments, he ironically causes his own death. This action demonstrates the bond of dependence between the hated double and the loved self. The murder-suicide confirms the double as the narrator's alter ego. In other words, the narrator's double exists not as an external character but rather as part of the narrator's imagination. Poe uses the idea of the double to question the narrator's grasp on reality. The murder-suicide implies that the narrator has imagined the existence of his rival because he suffers from paranoia, a mental state in which the human mind suspects itself to be threatened by external forces that are just imaginary figments of irs own creation.

LADY LIGEIA

Many women return from the dead in Poe's stories, and Lady Ligeia is the most alluring of them all. Ligeia's sudden reappearance casts doubt on the mental stability of her husband, the tale's narrator. Poe does not focus on the narrator's unreliability but instead develops the character of the dark and brilliant Ligeia. Ligeia's dark features contrast with those of the narrator's second wife, the fair-skinned and blonde Lady Rowena. Ligeia does not disappear from the story after her apparent death. In order to watch over her husband and his cold new bride, Ligeia becomes part of the Gothic architecture of the bridal chamber. Poe symbolically translates Ligeia's dark, haunting physical qualities into the Gothic and grotesque elements of the bedroom, including the eerie gold tapestries that Rowena believes comes alive. Ligeia is not only one of the dead who come alive but also a force that makes physical objects come alive. She uses these forces to doom the narrator's second marriage, and her manifestations in the architecture of the bedroom, whether real or the product of the narrator and his wife's imaginations, testify to the power of past emotions to influence the present and the future.

Themes, Motifs & Symbols

Themes

Themes are the fundamental and often universal ideas explored in a literary work.

Love and Hate

Poe explores the similarity of love and hate in many stories, especially "The Tell-Tale Heart" and "William Wilson." Poe portrays the psychological complexity of these two supposedly opposite emotions, emphasizing the ways they enigmatically blend into each other. Poe's psychological insight anticipates the theories of Sigmund Freud, the Austrian founder of psychoanalysis and one of the twentieth century's most influential thinkers. Poe, like Freud, interpreted love and hate as universal emotions, thereby severed from the specific conditions of time and space.

The Gothic terror is the result of the narrator's simultaneous love for himself and hatred of his rival. The double shows that love and hate are inseparable and suggests that they may simply be two forms of the most intense form of human emotion. The narrator loves himself, but when feelings of self-hatred arise in him, he projects that hatred onto an imaginary copy of himself. In "The Tell-Tale Heart," the narrator confesses a love for an old man whom he then violently murders and dismembers. The narrator reveals his madness by attempting to separate the person of the old man, whom he loves, from the old man's supposedly evil eye, which triggers the narrator's hatred. This delusional separation enables the narrator to remain unaware of the paradox of claiming to have loved his victim.

Self vs. Alter Ego

In many of Poe's Gothic tales, characters wage internal conflicts by creating imaginary alter egos or assuming alternate and opposite personalities. In "William Wilson," the divided self takes the form of the narrator's imagined double, who tracks him throughout Europe. The rival threatens the narrator's sense of a coherent identity because he demonstrates that it is impossible for him to escape his unwanted characteristics. The narrator uses the alter ego to separate himself from his insanity. He projects his inner turmoil onto his alter ego and is able to forget that the trouble resides within him. The alter ego becomes a rival of the self because its resemblance to the self is unmistakable. Suicide results from the delusion that the alter ego is something real that can be eliminated in order to leave the self in peace. In "The Black Cat" the narrator transforms from a gentle animal lover into an evil cat-killer. The horror of "The Black Cat" derives from this sudden transformation and the cruel act—the narrator's killing of his cat Pluto—which accompanies it. Pluto's reincarnation as the second cat haunts the narrator's guilty conscience. Although the narrator wants to forget his murder of Pluto, gallows appear in the color of his fur. The fur symbolizes the suppressed guilt that drives him insane and causes him to murder his wife.

THE POWER OF THE DEAD OVER THE LIVING

Poe often gives memory the power to keep the dead alive. Poe distorts this otherwise commonplace literary theme by bringing the dead literally back to life, employing memory as the trigger that reawakens the dead, who are usually women. In "Ligeia," the narrator cannot escape memories of his first wife, Ligeia, while his second wife, the lady Rowena, begins to suffer from a mysterious sickness. While the narrator's memories belong only to his own mind, Poe allows these memories to exert force in the physical world. Ligeia dies, but her husband's memory makes him see her in the architecture of the bedroom he shares with his new wife. In this sense, Gothic terror becomes a love story. The loving memory of a grieving husband revives a dead wife. "Ligeia" breaks down the barrier between life and death, but not just to scare the reader. Instead, the memory of the dead shows the power of love to resist even the permanence of death.

THEMES

MOTIFS

Motifs are recurring structures, contrasts, or literary devices that can help to develop and inform the text's major themes.

THE MASQUERADE

At masquerades Poe's characters abandon social conventions and leave themselves vulnerable to crime. In "The Cask of Amontillado," for example, Montresor uses the carnival's masquerade to fool Fortunato into his own demise. The masquerade carries the traditional meanings of joy and social liberation. Reality is suspended, and people can temporarily assume another identity. Montresor exploits these sentiments to do Fortunato real harm. In "William Wilson," the masquerade is where the narrator receives his double's final insult. The masquerade is enchanting because guests wear a variety of exotic and grotesque costumes, but the narrator and his double don the same Spanish outfit. The double Wilson haunts the narrator by denying him the thrill of unique transformation. In a crowd full of guests in costumes, the narrator feels comfortably anonymous enough to attempt to murder his double. Lastly, in "The Masque of the Red Death," the ultimate victory of the plague over the selfish retreat of Prince Prospero and his guests occurs during the palace's lavish masquerade ball. The mysterious guest's gruesome costume, which shows the bloody effects of the Red Death, mocks the larger horror of Prospero's party in the midst of his suffering peasants. The pretense of costume allows the guest to enter the ball, and bring the guests their death in person.

ANIMALS

In Poe's murder stories, homicide requires animalistic element. Animals kill, they die, and animal imagery provokes and informs crimes committed between men. Animals signal the absence of human reason and morality, but sometimes humans prove less rational than their beastly counterparts. The joke behind "The Murders in the Rue Morgue" is that the Ourang-Outang did it. The savage irrationality of the crime baffles the police, who cannot conceive of a motiveless crime or fathom the brute force involved. Dupin uses his superior analytical abilities to determine that the crime couldn't have been committed by a human. In "The Black Cat," the murder of Pluto results from the narrator's loss of reason and plunge into "perverseness," reason's inhuman antithesis. The story's second cat behaves cunningly, leading the narrator into a more serious crime in the murder of his wife, and then betraying him to the police. The role reversal—irrational humans vs. rational animals—indicates that Poe considers murder a fundamentally animalistic, and therefore inhuman, act. In "The Tell-Tale Heart," the murderer dehumanize his victims by likening him to animal. The narrator of "The Tell-Tale Heart" claims to hate and murder the old man's "vulture eye," which he describes as "pale blue with a film over it." He attempts to justify his actions by implicitly comparing himself to a helpless creature threatened by a hideous scavenger. In the "Cask of Amontillado," Montresor does the reverse, readying himself to commit the crime by equating himself with an animal. In killing Fortunato, he cites his family arms, a serpent with its fangs in the heel of a foot stepping on it, and motto, which is translated "no one harms me with impunity." Fortunato, whose insult has spurred Montresor to revenge, becomes the man whose foot harms the snake Montresor and is punished with a lethal bite.

SYMBOLS

Symbols are objects, characters, figures, or colors used to represent abstract ideas or concepts.

THE WHIRLPOOL

In "MS. Found in a Bottle," the whirlpool symbolizes insanity. When the whirlpool transports the narrator from the peaceful South Seas to the surreal waters of the South Pole, it also symbolically transports him out of the space of scientific rationality to that of the imaginative fancy of the German moralists. The whirlpool destroys the boat and removes the narrator from a realistic realm, the second whirlpool kills him.

EYES

In "The Tell-Tale Heart," the narrator fixates on the idea that an old man is looking at him with the Evil Eye and transmitting a curse on him. At the same time that the narrator obsesses over the eye, he wants to separate the old man from the Evil Eye in order to spare the old man from his violent reaction to the eye. The narrator reveals his inability to recognize that the "eye" is the "I," or identity, of the old man. The eyes symbolize the essence of human identity, which cannot be separated from the body. The eye cannot be killed without causing the man to die. Similarly, in "Ligeia," the narrator is unable to see behind Ligeia's dark and mysterious eyes. Because the eyes symbolize her Gothic identity, they conceal Ligeia's mysterious knowledge, a knowledge that both guides and haunts the narrator.

"FORTUNATO"

In "The Cask of Amontillado," Poe uses Fortunato's name symbolically, as an ironic device. Though his name means "the fortunate one" in Italian, Fortunato meets an unfortunate fate as the victim of Montresor's revenge. Fortunato adds to the irony of his name by wearing the costume of a court jester. While Fortunato plays in jest, Montresor sets out to fool him, with murderous results.

SYMBOLS

Summary & Analysis

"MS. Found in a Bottle" (1833)

Summary

An unnamed narrator frames his story by disclaiming connection to his family and country. He says that he prefers the company of the German moralist writers, whose flights of fancy he can detect and repudiate. He admits having a rigidly rational mindset, dedicated to the truth and impervious to superstition.

The narrator then recounts a voyage from the island of Java upon a vessel containing cotton-wool, cocoa-nuts, and a few cases of opium. Soon after departure, the narrator observes a large, ominous cloud in the distance and fears the signs of an approaching Simoon, or typhoon. The captain of the ship, however, dismisses the narrator's fears. As he retreats below deck, the narrator hears a loud noise and feels the ship capsizing. When the ship bobs back up, the narrator realizes that he and an old Swede are the only survivors. However, the ship remains engulfed in a whirlpool, which threatens to suck the vessel into the depths of the sea. For five days, the two men float on the shattered ship, escaping the pull of the whirlpool. They find their surroundings have grown cold, and soon complete darkness overwhelms them.

Another hurricane erupts amid this darkness, and the men observe a gigantic black ship riding on the crest of a large wave. The force of this ship's descent into the water rocks the narrator's ship and hurls him onto the unknown vessel. He quickly hides in the hold, where he observes the ancient mariners on the ship speaking an unrecognizable language. Growing braver, he explores the captain's private cabin, in which he finds the paper for the present manuscript. He proposes to enclose the manuscript in a bottle and toss it to sea.

The narrator then recounts a chance event in which he playfully dabbles with a tar brush on a folded sail. When spread out, the sail reads DISCOVERY. This event causes the narrator to examine the ship more closely. He is unsure of the ship's purpose, and its timber is oddly porous. Moreover, the members of the crew seem incapable of

seeing the narrator. Even the aged captain pays him no atten-
tion.The narrator continues on the ship in eternal darkness and
soon discovers that it is heading due south, perhaps destined for the
South Pole. As the excitement of discovery fills the crew and the narrator, the ice suddenly breaks apart to reveal a powerful whirlpool.
The pull of the vortex is too powerful for the ship to resist, and it is
sucked into the sea's black hole.

ANALYSIS

"MS. Found in a Bottle" initially appeared in the October 19,
1833 edition of a Baltimore newspaper, the *Saturday Visiter,* as the
winner of a literary contest for the best short tale. Poe had submit-
ted six tales to the *Visiter,* and the newspaper received over one
hundred submissions in all. Though the *Visiter* praised all of Poe's
entries, it singled out "MS. Found in a Bottle" for its expansive
imagination and its singular demonstration of learning. The *Visiter*
encouraged Poe to publish the entire volume. Following this
advice, Poe put together *Tales of the Grotesque and Arabesque*
over the next several years, and published the collection in 1840.

"MS. Found in a Bottle" was an early bright spot in Poe's literary
career, and it helped make his reputation, especially in Baltimore.
Poe originally grouped it in a larger volume, *Eleven Tales of the Arabesque,* to which he later added the category of the "grotesque."
This classification points to a distinction in Poe's writing between an
arabesque story—with themes derived from Near Eastern literature—such as "MS. Found in a Bottle," and a grotesque story—in
which "terror arises from the return to life by the dead"—like
"Ligeia." According to the 1840 preface to *Tales of the Grotesque
and Arabesque,* the grotesque relies upon human interaction, even
when monsters and figures from the dead animate the plot. The arabesque, on the other hand, deals with the horror of ideas and the
mysterious allure of cryptic patterns.

"MS. Found in a Bottle" is also one of Poe's most celebrated stories of science fiction. Poe was fascinated by the South Pole, and he
obsessively read the journals of Alexander von Humboldt, a German contemporary of Poe who traveled all over the world as part of
his cosmological research. Poe became interested in the fantastic
notion of a hole in the South Pole that emptied out to the other side
of the globe. The image of the whirlpool—and its power to shut
down the narrative—marks the South Pole as a threatening region

beyond human rationality and knowledge. Poe so enjoyed this line of narrative that he returned to it in subsequent stories. He expanded his treatment of the South Pole in his 1838 novel *The Narrative of Arthur Gordon Pym,* an adventure story of spying, mutiny, and exploration that culminates in the irrational engulfing whiteness of a whirlpool near the South Pole.

The horror of "MS. Found in a Bottle" comes from its scientific imaginings and its description of a physical world beyond the limits of human exploration. It emphasizes ideas, calling us back to the introduction of the story, in which the narrator announces his allegiance to realism. That realism is lost with the descent into the whirlpool, as, presumably, is the narrator's life.

The British Romantic poet Samuel Taylor Coleridge described a similar voyage into the unknown in his poem "The Rime of the Ancient Mariner." By stepping onto the ship of elderly sailors, Poe's narrator participates in a similar journey. Coleridge's mariner traveled south into the unknown and returned scarred and altered by the experience, with greater knowledge of the inner self. Poe's narrator looks deeper into his own self through the course of the narrative and grows ashamed of his former self. We learn nothing, however, of any return but only receive the manuscript placed in the bottle, where the narrator's story survives after he, presumably, is consumed by the whirlpool.

"LIGEIA" (1838)

> *I cannot, for my soul, remember how, when, or even precisely where, I first became acquainted with the lady Ligeia.*
>
> (See QUOTATIONS, p. 64)

SUMMARY

An unnamed narrator opens the story by claiming not to remember the circumstances in which he met his beloved, the lady Ligeia. Although he fixates on her rare learning, her unusual beauty, and her love of language, the narrator cannot specifically recall how Ligeia became his love object. He does speculate, however, that he first encountered her in Germany, where her family lived in an ancient city on the Rhine. He is confident that Ligeia spoke frequently about her family, but he does not believe he ever knew her last name.

The narrator counteracts this ignorance of Ligeia's origins with a faithful memory of her person. According to the narrator, Ligeia is tall, slender, and, in her later days, emaciated. She treads lightly, moving like a shadow. Though fiercely beautiful, Ligeia does not conform to a traditional mold of beauty: the narrator identifies a "strangeness" in her features. Ligeia's most distinctive feature is her hair—black as a raven and naturally curly. Among her physical features, only her brilliant black eyes rival her hair. They conceal the great knowledge and understanding Ligeia possesses and shares with the narrator. The narrator relishes his memory of her beauty but loves her learned mind even more passionately. She has guided him, during the early years of their marriage, through the chaotic world of his metaphysical studies.

As time passes, Ligeia becomes mysteriously ill. On the day of her death, she begs the narrator to read a poem she has composed about the natural tragedy of life. The poem describes a theater where angels have gathered to watch the mysterious actions of mimes, which are controlled by formless, outside presences. Suddenly, amid the drama, a creature intrudes and feeds on the mimes. With the fall of the curtain, the angels reveal that the tragedy is entitled "Man," and the hero is the creature, the Conqueror Worm. With the close of the poem, Ligeia shrieks a prayer about the unfairness of the tragedy and dies.

Devastated by Ligeia's death, the narrator moves to England and purchases an abbey. He soon marries again, this time to the fair, blue-eyed Lady Rowena Trevanion of Tremaine. The narrator's bridal chamber is a Gothic masterpiece, which includes a large window that lets in ghastly rays, a vaulted ceiling, various Eastern knickknacks, and large gold tapestries that hang from the walls. In this bridal chamber, the narrator and Lady Rowena spend the first month of their marriage. During that period, the narrator realizes that Rowena does not love him. At the beginning of the second month, Lady Rowena, like Ligeia, becomes mysteriously ill. Although she recovers temporarily, she reveals a hypersensitivity to sounds and an unexplained fear of the gold tapestries, which she fears are alive.

Lady Rowena's health takes a turn for the worse, and the narrator fears that her death is imminent. Sitting by her bed, he watches her drink a glass of wine, into which mysteriously fall, according to the narrator, three or four large drops of a red fluid. The narrator is unsure of his observations because he has recently smoked opium, to which he has become addicted during his second marriage. Three days later, Rowena dies, and on the fourth day, the narrator sits alone with her corpse but cannot keep his mind from the memories of Ligeia. Later that night, the narrator wakes to moans from Rowena's deathbed, and he discovers that a tinge of color has returned to Rowena's face. Rowena still lives. A second round of moans ensues, and the body reveals more color. However, the flash of life is brief, and Rowena's body becomes icy cold again.

Faced again with memories of Ligeia, the narrator, horrified, encounters another reawakening of the corpse. This time, however, the corpse moves from its deathbed and advances, shrouded, into the middle of the apartment. Aghast, the narrator mysteriously questions the identity of the corpse. Though he feels it must be the lady Rowena, he notices the body has grown taller. Glancing from her feet to her head, the narrator discovers raven-black hair emerging from behind the shroud—it is the lady Ligeia standing in the bridal chamber.

Analysis

"Ligeia" is Poe's most successful attempt to merge the Gothic grotesque with the traditional love story, elements also combined in "Berenice" and "Morella." Ligeia gives the story its name, and every detail of the plot draws its purpose from her character because she is the object of the narrator's love. Ligeia perseveres in spite of the obstacles—death and light—that Poe, as the author, places in her way. Ligeia dies, but her memory remains the primary fixation of the narrator's mind. The blonde-haired Rowena replaces her as the narrator's wife, but the darkness of the marriage bedroom suffocates the blonde, and Ligeia returns in Rowena's body, imbuing the blonde's body with her darker tones.

Poe contrasts light and darkness to symbolize the conflict of two philosophical traditions. Ligeia emerges mysteriously from the Rhine, a river in southwest Germany. Being German, she symbolizes the Germanic Romantic tradition, closely related to the Gothic, that embraced the sensual and the supernatural. Ligeia's mind is the center of the irrational and mystical, not the rational. The cold Lady Rowena is an ice queen from the north. She represents rationality. Rowena embodies the austerity and coldness of English empiricism, a philosophical tradition based on rational methods of observation, calculation, and analysis.

Rowena suffers from her confinement within a Gothic bridal chamber that is dark and filled with unnatural decorations. The narrator preserves Ligeia's sensuality and Romanticism's artificiality in the chamber's architecture and decorations. Rowena fears the red drops and the gold tapestries because they seem so unreal. Figuratively, Rowena dies because she is deprived of sunlight and nature. If the grotesque chamber is, in part, responsible for Rowena's death, then the lady Ligeia can be considered a symbolic accomplice.

Ligeia's ultimate victory is her return from the dead. Ligeia's return confirms that the narrator has lost his power's of rationality and lost touch with reality. Though some critics emphasize the unreliability of the narrator because of his abuse of opium, Poe is less concerned with the quality of the narrator's senses than with the power of his visions—what he sees, not how he sees it. This is not to say that Poe undervalues the narrator or means for us naïvely to believe his bizarre and contradictory confessions. Whether or not Ligeia's return from the dead is actually, physically real or an opium-induced delusion, her apparent physical manifestation at the end of the story means that she has become more real for the narrator than a memory.

Many of Poe's narrator's are unreliable because of paranoia and guilt about their own crimes, as in "The Black Cat," in which the narrator is anxious about the discovery of his murder. In "Ligeia," the narrator is obsessed with lost love. His love embraces contradictions. For instance, he passionately loves a woman without knowing her last name. But for Poe, these contradictions are symptoms of love. Poe offers the possibility that love brings Ligeia back, if only in the eyes of the narrator. The mysteriousness of Ligeia's eyes spreads symbolically to the narrator's eyes. If Ligeia conceals vast knowledge behind her eyes, then the narrator somehow inherits her eyes' power to take in unnatural knowledge—to see the dead. The difference lies in the narrator's ability to convey his knowledge to us, allowing us to witness and judge the return of the lady Ligeia. Neither we nor the narrator ever saw what was behind Ligeia's eyes, and their mystery lent them their allure.

While "Ligeia" strives to be a love story, it relies heavily on the sort of Gothic imagery for which Poe became famous. "Ligeia" resembles a criminal story like "The Tell-Tale Heart" with its emphasis on the narrator's obsession with specific body parts. Eyes are crucial to both stories, and in this tale, Ligeia's hair takes on the same importance. The Gothic dimension of this obsession involves the fantasy of reducing a human being to her body parts. The Gothic emphasis on anatomy raises the possibility that aspects of human identity reside in specific body parts, throwing into question the notion of an immortal soul. What survives of Ligeia is not her soul, but the materialized form of her body, conveyed symbolically, in the last scene of the tale, by her dark hair. The story only dramatizes the unconscious longings of the narrator to see his lost love again, and it gives these longings the physical shape of Ligeia's body. The love story, then, reverses the murder and dismemberment of a horror story like "The Tell-Tale Heart." Love becomes the ability to revive a dead body.

"THE FALL OF THE HOUSE OF USHER" (1839)

> *A striking similitude between the brother and the sister now first arrested my attention. . . .*
>
> (See QUOTATIONS, p. 65)

SUMMARY

An unnamed narrator approaches the house of Usher on a "dull, dark, and soundless day." This house—the estate of his boyhood friend, Roderick Usher—is gloomy and mysterious. The narrator observes that the house seems to have absorbed an evil and diseased atmosphere from the decaying trees and murky ponds around it. He notes that although the house is decaying in places—individual stones are disintegrating, for example—the structure itself is fairly solid. There is only a small crack from the roof to the ground in the front of the building. He has come to the house because his friend Roderick sent him a letter earnestly requesting his company. Roderick wrote that he was feeling physically and emotionally ill, so the narrator is rushing to his assistance. The narrator mentions that the Usher family, though an ancient clan, has never flourished. Only one member of the Usher family has survived from generation to generation, thereby forming a direct line of descent without any outside branches. The Usher family has become so identified with its estate that the peasantry confuses the inhabitants with their home.

The narrator finds the inside of the house just as spooky as the outside. He makes his way through the long passages to the room where Roderick is waiting. He notes that Roderick is paler and less energetic than he once was. Roderick tells the narrator that he suffers from nerves and fear and that his senses are heightened. The narrator also notes that Roderick seems afraid of his own house. Roderick's sister, Madeline, has taken ill with a mysterious sickness—perhaps catalepsy, the loss of control of one's limbs—that the doctors cannot reverse. The narrator spends several days trying to cheer up Roderick. He listens to Roderick play the guitar and make up words for his songs, and he reads him stories, but he cannot lift Roderick's spirit. Soon, Roderick posits his theory that the house itself is unhealthy, just as the narrator supposes at the beginning of the story.

Madeline soon dies, and Roderick decides to bury her temporarily in the tombs below the house. He wants to keep her in the house because he fears that the doctors might dig up her body for scientific examination, since her disease was so strange to them. The narrator helps Roderick put the body in the tomb, and he notes that Madeline has rosy cheeks, as some do after death. The narrator also realizes suddenly that Roderick and Madeline were twins. Over the next few days, Roderick becomes even more uneasy. One night, the narrator cannot sleep either. Roderick knocks on his door, apparently hysterical. He leads the narrator to the window, from which they see a bright-looking gas surrounding the house. The narrator tells Roderick that the gas is a natural phenomenon, not altogether uncommon.

The narrator decides to read to Roderick in order to pass the night away. He reads "Mad Trist" by Sir Launcelot Canning, a medieval romance. As he reads, he hears noises that correspond to the descriptions in the story. At first, he ignores these sounds as the vagaries of his imagination. Soon, however, they become more distinct and he can no longer ignore them. He also notices that Roderick has slumped over in his chair and is muttering to himself. The narrator approaches Roderick and listens to what he is saying. Roderick reveals that he has been hearing these sounds for days, and believes that they have buried Madeline alive and that she is trying to escape. He yells that she is standing behind the door. The wind blows open the door and confirms Roderick's fears: Madeline stands in white robes bloodied from her struggle. She attacks Roderick as the life drains from her, and he dies of fear. The narrator flees the house. As he escapes, the entire house cracks along the break in the frame and crumbles to the ground.

ANALYSIS

"The Fall of the House of Usher" possesses the quintessential features of the Gothic tale: a haunted house, dreary landscape, mysterious sickness, and doubled personality. For all its easily identifiable Gothic elements, however, part of the terror of this story is its vagueness. We cannot say for sure where in the world or exactly when the story takes place. Instead of standard narrative markers of place and time, Poe uses traditional Gothic elements such as inclement weather and a barren landscape. We are alone with the narrator in this haunted space, and neither we nor the narrator know why. Although he is Roderick's most intimate boyhood friend, the narrator apparently does not know much about him—like the basic fact that Roderick has a twin sister. Poe asks us to question the reasons both for Roderick's decision to contact the narrator in this time of need and the bizarre tenacity of narrator's response. While Poe provides the recognizable building blocks of the Gothic tale, he contrasts this standard form with a plot that is inexplicable, sudden, and full of unexpected disruptions. The story begins without complete explanation of the narrator's motives for arriving at the house of Usher, and this ambiguity sets the tone for a plot that continually blurs the real and the fantastic.

Poe creates a sensation of claustrophobia in this story. The narrator is mysteriously trapped by the lure of Roderick's attraction, and he cannot escape until the house of Usher collapses completely. Characters cannot move and act freely in the house because of its structure, so it assumes a monstrous character of its own—the Gothic mastermind that controls the fate of its inhabitants. Poe, creates confusion between the living things and inanimate objects by doubling the physical house of Usher with the genetic family line of the Usher family, which he refers to as the house of Usher. Poe employs the word "house" metaphorically, but he also describes a real house. Not only does the narrator get trapped inside the mansion, but we learn also that this confinement describes the biological fate of the Usher family. The family has no enduring branches, so all genetic transmission has occurred incestuously within the domain of the house. The peasantry confuses the mansion with the family because the physical structure has effectively dictated the genetic patterns of the family.

The claustrophobia of the mansion affects the relations among characters. For example, the narrator realizes late in the game that Roderick and Madeline are twins, and this realization occurs as the two men prepare to entomb Madeline. The cramped and confined setting of the burial tomb metaphorically spreads to the features of the characters. Because the twins are so similar, they cannot develop as free individuals. Madeline is buried before she has actually died because her similarity to Roderick is like a coffin that holds her identity. Madeline also suffers from problems typical for women in nineteenth-century literature. She invests all of her identity in her body, whereas Roderick possesses the powers of intellect. In spite of this disadvantage, Madeline possesses the power in the story, almost superhuman at times, as when she breaks out of her tomb. She thus counteracts Roderick's weak, nervous, and immobile disposition. Some scholars have argued that Madeline does not even exist, reducing her to a shared figment Roderick's and the narrator's imaginations. But Madeline proves central to the symmetrical and claustrophobic logic of the tale. Madeline stifles Roderick by preventing him from seeing himself as essentially different from her. She completes this attack when she kills him at the end of the story.

Doubling spreads throughout the story. The tale highlights the Gothic feature of the doppelganger, or character double, and portrays doubling in inanimate structures and literary forms. The narrator, for example, first witnesses the mansion as a reflection in the tarn, or shallow pool, that abuts the front of the house. The mirror image in the tarn doubles the house, but upside down—an inversely symmetrical relationship that also characterizes the relationship between Roderick and Madeline.

The story features numerous allusions to other works of literature, including the poems "The Haunted Palace" and "Mad Trist" by Sir Launcelot Canning. Poe composed them himself and then fictitiously attributed them to other sources. Both poems parallel and thus predict the plot line of "The Fall of the House of Usher." "Mad Trist," which is about the forceful entrance of Ethelred into the dwelling of a hermit, mirrors the simultaneous escape of Madeline from her tomb. "Mad Trist" spookily crosses literary borders, as though Roderick's obsession with these poems ushers their narratives into his own domain and brings them to life.

The crossing of borders pertains vitally to the Gothic horror of the tale. We know from Poe's experience in the magazine industry that he was obsessed with codes and word games, and this story amplifies his obsessive interest in naming. "Usher" refers not only to the mansion and the family, but also to the act of crossing a threshold that brings the narrator into the perverse world of Roderick and

Madeline. Roderick's letter ushers the narrator into a world he does not know, and the presence of this outsider might be the factor that destroys the house. The narrator is the lone exception to the Ushers' fear of outsiders, a fear that accentuates the claustrophobic nature of the tale. By undermining this fear of the outside, the narrator unwittingly brings down the whole structure. A similar, though strangely playful crossing of a boundary transpires both in "Mad Trist" and during the climactic burial escape, when Madeline breaks out from death to meet her mad brother in a "tryst," or meeting, of death. Poe thus buries, in the fictitious gravity of a medieval romance, the puns that garnered him popularity in America's magazines.

"WILLIAM WILSON" (1839)

"In me didst thou exist—and, in my death, see by this image, which is thine own, how utterly thou hast murdered thyself." (See QUOTATIONS, p. 62)

SUMMARY

An unnamed narrator announces that his real name shall remain a mystery, for he wishes to preserve the purity of the page before him. Instead, the narrator asks that we know him as "William Wilson" throughout the tale of misery and crime that he is about to tell. He explains that this tale will explain his sudden and complete turn to evil.

The narrator believes that he has inherited an excitable temperament from his otherwise dull-minded parents. As a young student, he escapes from this environment, and his early memories concern a large Elizabethan house in England where he attended school. He describes the school as a Gothic prison, with a spiked iron gate that has creaky hinges. The principal, who also acts as the pastor of the church, enforces the severe rules of the school.

Despite the severity of his surroundings, the narrator emerges as a colorful student and feels a certain superiority to his classmates, with the exception of one student. According to the narrator, this student bears exactly the same name: William Wilson. This second William Wilson interferes with the narrator's mastery over his classmates, thereby becoming for the narrator an object of fear and competition. This rivalry becomes only more pronounced for the narrator when he learns that they joined the school on the same day and that, because of the two William Wilsons' identical builds and styles of dress, many older students believe they are brothers. The narrator's rival even imitates his mode of speaking, except he can never raise his voice above a whisper. Nevertheless, the narrator rejects any connection between him and his rival. Despite this antagonism, though, the narrator remains on speaking terms with his competitor and admits, at first, to being unable to hate him.

The relationship soon deteriorates, however, and a violent altercation ensues between the two William Wilsons. The scuffle evokes in the narrator memories of his infancy, which makes him grow only more obsessed with William Wilson. On a night not long after the scuffle, the narrator sneaks into his rival's bedroom to play a practical joke. Shining the light from his lamp on his rival's face, the narrator believes he sees a different William Wilson, a face unique to the darkness. Terrified by the facial transformation he imagines, the narrator rushes from the room.

After several months, the narrator becomes a student at another school, Eton, and attempts to leave behind memories of the other William Wilson. He abuses alcohol in this effort to forget the past, and he recalls one debaucherous party in particular. In the midst of the drunken revelry, a servant announces the presence of a mysterious guest calling for the attention of the narrator. Excited and intoxicated, the narrator rushes to the vestibule, only to discover a youth of his same size and dress. The faintness of the light prevents the narrator from discerning the visitor's face. Grabbing the narrator's arm, the guest whispers "William Wilson" in the narrator's ear and quickly vanishes.

Changing schools again, the narrator moves to Oxford, where he picks up the vice of gambling. Skilled at this vice, the narrator chooses weak-minded classmates on whom to prey for extravagant monetary gain. After two years at Oxford, the narrator meets a young nobleman named Glendinning and makes him his next gambling target. Allowing him to win at first, the narrator lures him with the prospect of more success to a large party he has arranged. At this party, Glendinning plays exactly as the narrator expects and quickly amasses large debts. At the moment that he quadruples his debt, Glendinning becomes ghastly pale, and the narrator realizes his triumph. Suddenly, however, a stranger intrudes on the party with a rush that extinguishes all the candles in the room. He reveals the narrator to be a scam artist and promptly retreats. The announcement ruins the narrator, forcing his departure not only from Oxford, but also from Britain.

Settling at last in Rome, the narrator attends a masquerade ball in the palace of the duke Di Broglio. The narrator secretly desires the wife of the duke, who has informed him of the costume she will be wearing. As he searches for her, the narrator feels a light hand on his arm and hears a whisper in his ear: "William Wilson." The whisperer wears the same costume as the narrator, a Spanish cloak with a black silk mask. Drawn into a side room, the narrator becomes enraged, drawing his sword and stabbing his rival. To the narrator's horror, the layout of the room mysteriously changes, and a mirror replaces the body of his antagonist. He stares into the mirror to find his own body stabbed and bleeding, and he hears his rival speak as though with his own voice: "In me didst thou exist—and, in my death, see by this image, which is thine own, how utterly thou hast murdered thyself."

Analysis

"William Wilson" is Poe's most sustained character study of the doppelganger, or double, a theme explored in a similar way recently by the popular film *Fight Club*. Poe doubles the twins Roderick and Madeline Usher in "The Fall of the House of Usher" and in "William Wilson." While Poe focuses on Roderick and Madeline's physical relationship in "The Fall of the House of Usher," he is interested in the psychological self-splitting that produces the two William Wilsons in "William Wilson." Although Poe's focus is undoubtedly the alter ego—the part of the self that haunts us against our will—he portrays this psychological condition through the manifestation of another body. The final image of the murder-suicide points to the ultimate inseparability of body and mind. The narrator may be plagued mentally and intellectually by his rivalrous double, but he can register his revenge only in physical, corporeal terms, such as the thrust of his sword that carries with it the angst of his tortured mind.

Poe's study of psychology in "William Wilson" anticipates the major theories of Sigmund Freud, the founder of psychoanalysis and one of the twentieth century's most important psychologists. Poe's notion of the rivalrous double predates Freud's concept of the repressed, unconscious alter ego by at least half a century. Like Freud, Poe associates the alter ego with a universal psychological condition, unaffected by specifics of time or place. William Wilson's double follows him across Europe—from England to Italy—and from childhood to adult life. It is clear that the narrator's mental splitting of himself into two William Wilsons does not result from aggravating factors of a specific environment, since the narrator purposefully moves to different environments in an attempt to elude his double. The doppelganger represents the narrator's attempt to project an inner evil on the outside world. Whereas "The Tell-Tale Heart" shows how the mad narrator internally fixates on something external—the old man's eye—"William Wilson" portrays the reverse of this psychological trajectory.

Like "The Tell-Tale Heart," "William Wilson" thematically explores the ambiguous doubling of love and hate. As much as the narrator resists, he cannot help initially feeling affection for his rival. In fact, the tale's murderous resolution shows how necessary the hated alter ego is for the sustenance of life. Because the long-awaited murder of his double also constitutes the narrator's suicide, Poe suggests that we unwittingly thrive on those elements in life that we most want to reject. The inclination to reject or repress a set of emotions—like the hatred of a rival—indicates how important those emotions are to the self.

As in "The Masque of the Red Death" and "The Cask of Amontillado," the dramatic resolution of "William Wilson" occurs during a masquerade party. Poe relies upon the motif of the masquerade to set loose the homicidal impulses of the narrator. But he suggests that the narrator's original desire, though not murderous, is still less than virtuous: he wants to make romantic advances toward the young and beautiful wife of the aged duke. Poe connects lust with the narrator's obsession with his own identity. Poe exaggerates the rivalry by dressing the men in identical costumes, intimating that the narrator cannot escape his own demons, even when he dons a disguise. Only in service to his desire for the duchess does the narrator act on the animosity that has plagued him since childhood.

"THE MURDERS IN THE RUE MORGUE" (1841)

SUMMARY

An unnamed narrator begins this tale of murder and criminal detection with a discussion of the analytic mind. He describes the analyst as driven paradoxically by both intuition and the moral inclination to disentangle what confuses his peers. He adds that the analyst takes delight in mathematical study and in the game of checkers, which allows the calculating individual to practice the art of detection—not only of the moves integral to the game, but also the demeanor of his opponent. The narrator argues, however, that analysis is not merely ingenuity. He states that while the ingenious man may, at times, be analytic, the calculating man is, without fail, always imaginative.

The narrator then describes the circumstances in which he met a man named C. Auguste Dupin. Both men were searching for the same book at an obscure library in the Rue Montmartre, in Paris, and began to converse. Soon, they became friends and decided to share the expenses of a residence together. The narrator then relays an anecdote illustrating Dupin's brilliant powers of analysis: one night, while walking together, Dupin describes an actor whom the narrator is pondering. Amazed, the narrator asks Dupin to explain his method, and we witness Dupin's capacity to work backward and observe the importance of seemingly insignificant details in order to reach ingenious conclusions.

Soon thereafter, the narrator and Dupin read newspaper headlines about a horrible murder in the Rue Morgue. One night at three A.M., eight or ten neighbors of Madame L'Espanaye and her daughter, Mademoiselle Camille, wake to shrieks from their fourth-floor apartment. The neighbors hear two voices, then silence. The neighbors and two policemen finally break into the locked apartment to find utter disorder and multiple pieces of evidence of a crime, including a blood-smeared razor, locks of gray human hair, bags of money, and an opened safe. They find no traces of the older woman. However, the noticeable traces of soot in the room lead them to the chimney, where they find the corpse of Mademoiselle Camille. They reason that the murderer must have choked Camille to death and then thrust her body up into the chimney. Expanding the search, the neighbors and police discover the body of Madame L'Espanaye in a courtyard in the rear of the building. They find her badly beaten, with her throat severely cut. When the police move the body, in fact, her head falls off. The 4,000 francs that Madame L'Espanaye had just withdrawn from the bank are still in the apartment, ruling out robbery as a motive for the grisly crime.

The newspaper then recounts the depositions of witnesses concerning the voices they heard. They all agree that they heard two voices: one, a deep Frenchman's voice; and the other, a higher voice of uncertain ethnic origin, though speculated to be Spanish. The gender of the second speaker is uncertain. The same newspaper reports the findings of the medical examiner, who confirms that Camille died from choking and that Madame L'Espanaye was beaten to death with immense violence, most likely by a club. The evening edition of the paper reports a new development. The police have arrested Adolphe Le Bon, a bank clerk who once did Dupin a favor.

With the arrest of Le Bon, Dupin becomes interested in pursuing the investigation and obtains permission to search the crime scene. Dupin is eager to survey the setting because the newspaper reports portray the apartment as impossible to escape from the inside, which makes the case so mysterious. Dupin suggests that the police have been so distracted by the atrocity of the murder and the apparent lack of motive that, while they have been attentive to what has occurred, they have failed to consider that the present crime could be something that has never occurred before. Producing two pistols, Dupin reveals that he awaits the arrival of a person who will prove his solution to the crime.

Dupin also names those elements of the crime scene that he believes the police have mishandled. For example, the shrill voice remains unidentifiable in its gender and its nationality, but it also cannot be identified as emitting words at all, just sounds. He also explains that the police have overlooked the windows in the apartment, which operate by springs and can be opened from the inside. Though the police believe the windows to be nailed shut, Dupin discovers a broken nail in one window, which only seemed to be intact. Dupin surmises that someone could have opened the window, exited the apartment, and closed the window from the outside without raising suspicion.

Dupin also addresses the mode of entry through the windows. The police imagine that no suspect could climb up the walls to the point of entry. Dupin hypothesizes that a person or thing of great agility could leap from the lightning rod outside the window to the shutters of the window. Dupin surmises that no ordinary human could inflict the beating that Madame L'Espanaye suffered. The murderer would have to possess superhuman strength and inhuman ferocity. To satisfy the confusion of the narrator, Dupin points out that the hair removed from Madame L'Espanaye's fingers was not human hair. After drawing a picture of the size and shape of the hand that killed the two women, Dupin reveals his solution. The hand matches the paw of an Ourang-Outang.

Dupin has advertised the safe capture of the animal, news that he believes will draw out its owner. Dupin adds that the owner must be a sailor, since, at the base of the lightning rod, he found a ribbon knotted in a way unique to naval training.

When the sailor arrives, Dupin draws his pistol and demands all the information he knows about the murders. He assures the sailor that he believes him to be innocent. The sailor describes how the animal, grasping a razor, escaped from its closet one night and disappeared from his apartment. The sailor followed the Ourang-Outang and watched him climb the lightning rod and leap into the window. Because he does not possess the animal's agility, the sailor could only watch the animal as it slashed Madame L'Espanaye and choked Camille. Before escaping the apartment, the animal threw Madame L'Espanaye's body to the courtyard below. The sailor thus confirms the identity of the mysterious voices—the deep voice was his own, and the shrill shrieks were that of the Ourang-Outang.

When informed of Dupin's solution, the police release Le Bon. The prefect is unable to conceal his chagrin at being outwitted by Dupin. He is happy to have the crime solved, but he is sarcastic, rather than grateful, about Dupin's assistance. Dupin comments, in conclusion, that the prefect is a man of ingenuity, not analysis.

ANALYSIS

"The Murders in the Rue Morgue" introduces a new genre of short fiction to American literature: the detective story. The detective story emerged from Poe's long-standing interest in mind games, puzzles, and secret codes called cryptographs, which Poe regularly published and decoded in the pages of the *Southern Literary Messenger*. He would dare his readers to submit a code he could not decipher. More commonly, though, Poe created fake personalities who would send in puzzles that he solved. "The Murders in the Rue Morgue," along with the later story "The Purloined Letter," allows Poe to sustain a longer narrative in which he presents seemingly unsolvable conundrums that his hero, M. Auguste Dupin, can always ultimately master. Dupin becomes a stand-in for Poe, who constructs and solves an elaborate cryptograph in the form of a bizarre murder case.

Poe's life is also relevant to "The Murders in the Rue Morgue." The tale's murders involve two women, and Poe spent his adult life with his wife, Virginia, and his aunt, Maria "Muddy" Clemm. The deaths of women resonate with Poe's early childhood experience of watching his mother die and Francis Allan suffer. The chaotic and deathly Rue Morgue apartment symbolizes the personal tragedies involving women that afflicted Poe's life. Poe contrasts the violent disorder of Madame L'Espanaye's household with the calm domesticity that Dupin and the narrator experience. Poe never found, in his lifetime, this sort of household solace, and he invests this scene of domestic ruin with the poignant experiences of his own life. The creation of Dupin allows Poe not only to highlight his own remarkable cunning, but also to share in the domestic tranquility and fraternity that he long sought.

"The Murders in the Rue Morgue" also relies on the role of the narrator as Dupin's friend. Poe chooses not to use Dupin as a narrator in order to provide a sense of detachment from the workings of the mind that the story describes. The narrator's role as a foil enhances Dupin as the detective hero. The narrator admires Dupin and prompts him to elicit his analysis, which always astounds the narrator. He allows himself to be outwitted by Dupin, thereby demonstrating that Dupin thinks one step ahead of both the police and the average reader. Accompanying Dupin to the crime scene, the narrator ostensibly witnesses the same evidence, but needs the explanations of his friend in order to see the true nature of the evidence and to understand its part in the larger puzzle.

Part of Dupin's brilliance is his ability to separate himself from the emotional atrocity of the crime scene. The police become distracted by the sheer inhuman cruelty of the scene, but Dupin is able to look beyond the violence and coolly investigate the small details that otherwise go unnoticed. The decapitation of Madame L'Espanaye is just one ghastly example that, according to Dupin, draws the police away from solving the crime. For all of Dupin's rationality and cunning, though, the actual explanation of the crime is, by all accounts, ridiculous—the Ourang-Outang did it. It is difficult to discern whether he intended this solution to be humourous. If the story is to be construed in some way as a joke—the detective story was too young at this time to be parodied—it is a joke told with the straightest of faces. Poe's tendency to exaggerate gets the better of him in his effort to illustrate the analytic contrasts between Dupin and the Paris police. One can argue that Dupin's brilliance is ultimately overshadowed by the need to import a wild animal into the solution to the crime. Dupin gets the case right, but Poe may, in fact, go too far in exaggerating the power of his protagonist's reasoning.

"THE TELL-TALE HEART" (1843)

SUMMARY

An unnamed narrator opens the story by addressing the reader and claiming that he is nervous but not mad. He says that he is going to tell a story in which he will defend his sanity yet confess to having killed an old man. His motivation was neither passion nor desire for money, but rather a fear of the man's pale blue eye. Again, he insists that he is not crazy because his cool and measured actions, though criminal, are not those of a madman. Every night, he went to the old man's apartment and secretly observed the man sleeping. In the morning, he would behave as if everything were normal. After a week of this activity, the narrator decides, somewhat randomly, that the time is right actually to kill the old man.

When the narrator arrives late on the eighth night, though, the old man wakes up and cries out. The narrator remains still, stalking the old man as he sits awake and frightened. The narrator understands how frightened the old man is, having also experienced the lonely terrors of the night. Soon, the narrator hears a dull pounding that he interprets as the old man's terrified heartbeat. Worried that a neighbor might hear the loud thumping, he attacks and kills the old man. He then dismembers the body and hides the pieces below the floorboards in the bedroom. He is careful not to leave even a drop of blood on the floor. As he finishes his job, a clock strikes the hour of four. At the same time, the narrator hears a knock at the street door. The police have arrived, having been called by a neighbor who heard the old man shriek. The narrator is careful to be chatty and to appear normal. He leads the officers all over the house without acting suspiciously. At the height of his bravado, he even brings them into the old man's bedroom to sit down and talk at the scene of the crime. The policemen do not suspect a thing. The narrator is comfortable until he starts to hear a low thumping sound. He recognizes the low sound as the heart of the old man, pounding away beneath the floorboards. He panics, believing that the policemen must also hear the sound and know his guilt. Driven mad by the idea that they are mocking his agony with their pleasant chatter, he confesses to the crime and shrieks at the men to rip up the floorboards.

ANALYSIS

Poe uses his words economically in the "Tell-Tale Heart"—it is one of his shortest stories—to provide a study of paranoia and mental deterioration. Poe strips the story of excess detail as a way to heighten the murderer's obsession with specific and unadorned entities: the old man's eye, the heartbeat, and his own claim to sanity. Poe's economic style and pointed language thus contribute to the narrative content, and perhaps this association of form and content truly exemplifies paranoia. Even Poe himself, like the beating heart, is complicit in the plot to catch the narrator in his evil game.

As a study in paranoia, this story illuminates the psychological contradictions that contribute to a murderous profile. For example, the narrator admits, in the first sentence, to being dreadfully nervous, yet he is unable to comprehend why he should be thought mad. He articulates his self-defense against madness in terms of heightened sensory capacity. Unlike the similarly nervous and hypersensitive Roderick Usher in "The Fall of the House of Usher," who admits that he feels mentally unwell, the narrator of "The Tell-Tale Heart" views his hypersensitivity as proof of his sanity, not a symptom of madness. This special knowledge enables the narrator to tell this tale in a precise and complete manner, and he uses the stylistic tools of narration for the purposes of his own sanity plea. However, what makes this narrator mad—and most unlike Poe—is that he fails to comprehend the coupling of narrative form and content. He masters precise form, but he unwittingly lays out a tale of murder that betrays the madness he wants to deny.

Another contradiction central to the story involves the tension between the narrator's capacities for love and hate. Poe explores here a psychological mystery—that people sometimes harm those whom they love or need in their lives. Poe examines this paradox half a century before Sigmund Freud made it a leading concept in his theories of the mind. Poe's narrator loves the old man. He is not greedy for the old man's wealth, nor vengeful because of any slight. The narrator thus eliminates motives that might normally inspire such a violent murder. As he proclaims his own sanity, the narrator fixates on the old man's vulture-eye. He reduces the old man to the pale blue of his eye in obsessive fashion. He wants to separate the man from his "Evil Eye" so he can spare the man the burden of guilt that he attributes to the eye itself. The narrator fails to see that the eye is the "I" of the old man, an inherent part of his identity that cannot be isolated as the narrator perversely imagines.

The murder of the old man illustrates the extent to which the narrator separates the old man's identity from his physical eye. The narrator sees the eye as completely separate from the man, and as a result, he is capable of murdering him while maintaining that he loves him. The narrator's desire to eradicate the man's eye motivates his murder, but the narrator does not acknowledge that this act will end the man's life. By dismembering his victim, the narrator further deprives the old man of his humanity. The narrator confirms his conception of the old man's eye as separate from the man by ending the man altogether and turning him into so many parts. That strategy turns against him when his mind imagines other parts of the old man's body working against him.

The narrator's newly heightened sensitivity to sound ultimately overcomes him, as he proves unwilling or unable to distinguish between real and imagined sounds. Because of his warped sense of reality, he obsesses over the low beats of the man's heart yet shows little concern about the man's shrieks, which are loud enough both to attract a neighbor's attention and to draw the police to the scene of the crime. The police do not perform a traditional, judgmental role in this story. Ironically, they aren't terrifying agents of authority or brutality. Poe's interest is less in external forms of power than in the power that pathologies of the mind can hold over an individual. The narrator's paranoia and guilt make it inevitable that he will give himself away. The police arrive on the scene to give him the opportunity to betray himself. The more the narrator proclaims his own cool manner, the more he cannot escape the beating of his own heart, which he mistakes for the beating of the old man's heart. As he confesses to the crime in the final sentence, he addresses the policemen as "[v]illains," indicating his inability to distinguish between their real identity and his own villainy.

"THE PIT AND THE PENDULUM" (1843)

SUMMARY

An unnamed narrator opens the story by revealing that he has been sentenced to death during the time of the Inquisition—an institution of the Catholic government in fifteenth- and sixteenth-century Spain that persecuted all Protestants and heretical Catholics. Upon receiving his death sentence, the narrator swoons, losing consciousness. When he wakes, he faces complete darkness. He is confused because he knows that the usual fate of Inquisition victims is a pub-lic auto-da-fé, or "act of faith"—an execution normally taking the form of a hanging. He is afraid that he has been locked in a tomb, but he gets up and walks a few paces. This mobility then leads him to surmise that he is not in a tomb, but perhaps in one of the dun-geons at Toledo, an infamous Inquisition prison. He decides to explore. Ripping off a piece of the hem from his robe, he places it against the wall so that he can count the number of steps required to walk the perimeter of the cell. However, he soon stumbles and col-lapses to the ground, where he falls asleep.

Upon waking, the narrator finds offerings of water and bread, which he eagerly consumes. He then resumes his exploration of the prison, determining it to be roughly one hundred paces around. He decides to walk across the room. As he crosses, though, the hem that he ripped earlier tangles around his feet and trips him. Hitting the floor, he realizes that, although most of his body has fallen on solid ground, his face dangles over an abyss. To his dismay, he concludes that in the center of the prison there exists a circular pit. To estimate its depth, the narrator breaks a stone off the wall of the pit and throws it in, timing its descent. The pit, he believes, is quite deep, with water at the bottom. Reflecting upon his proximity to the pit, the narrator explains its function as a punishment of surprise, infa-mously popular with the Inquisitors. The narrator falls asleep again and wakes up to more water and bread. After drinking, he immedi-ately falls asleep again and imagines that the water must have been drugged. When he wakes up the next time, he finds the prison dimly lit. He remarks that he has overestimated its size, most likely having duplicated his steps during his explorations.

The narrator discovers that he is now bound to a wooden board by a long strap wrapped around his body. His captors offer him some flavorful meat in a dish, but no more water. When he looks up, he notices that the figure of Time has been painted on the ceiling. Time, however, has been made into a machine, specifically a pendu-lum, which appears to be swinging back and forth. The narrator looks away from the ceiling, though, when he notices rats coming out of the pit and swarming around his food. When he returns his focus to the ceiling, he discovers that the pendulum is constructed like a scythe and is making a razor-sharp crescent in its descent toward him. Its progress, however, is maddeningly slow and in a tra-jectory directly over his heart. Even though he recognizes how dire the situation is, the narrator remains hopeful. When the pendulum gets very close to him, he has a flash of insight. He rubs the food from his plate all over the strap that is restraining his mobility. Drawn by the food, the rats climb on top of the narrator and chew through the strap. As the pendulum nears his heart, the narrator breaks through the strap and escapes from the pendulum's swing. When he gets up, the pendulum retracts to the ceiling, and he concludes that people must be watching his every move.

The walls of the prison then heat up and begin moving in toward the pit. The narrator realizes that the enclosing walls will force him into the pit, an escape that will also mean his death. When there remains not even an inch foothold for the narrator, the walls suddenly retract and cool down. In his fear, however, the narrator has begun to faint into the pit. To his great surprise, though, a mysterious person latches onto him and prevents his fall. The French general Lasalle and his army have successfully taken over the prison in their effort to terminate the Inquisition.

ANALYSIS

"The Pit and the Pendulum" is distinct among Poe's first-person narrations. Unlike the hypersensitive characters from other stories, such as Roderick in "The Fall of the House of Usher" or the narrator in "The Tell-Tale Heart," this narrator claims to lose the capacity of sensation during the swoon that opens the story. He thus highlights his own unreliability in ways that other narrators resist or deny. Upon describing his possible loss of sensation, though, the narrator of "The Pit and the Pendulum" proceeds to convey the sensory details that he previously claims are beyond him. The narrative pattern resembles that of other stories, such as "The Tell-Tale Heart," to the extent that the narrator says and does the opposite of what he originally announces. This story diverges from the pattern, however, in that this narrator's descriptions are more objectively valid—that is, less concerned with proving the narrator's own sanity than with relaying and accounting for the elements of his incarceration. The story is also unusual among Poe's tales because it is hopeful. Hope is manifest in the story not only in the rescue that resolves the tale, but also in the tale's narrative strategy. The narrator maintains the capacity to recount faithfully and rationally his surroundings while also describing his own emotional turmoil. Unlike in "The Tell-Tale Heart," for example, the burden of emotional distress does not hinder storytelling.

"The Pit and the Pendulum" also stands out as one of Poe's most historically specific tales. Poe counteracts the placelessness of a story like "The Fall of the House of Usher" with the historical context of the Inquisition and its religious politics. This historical frame fills in for a personal history of the narrator. We do not know the specific circumstances of his arrest, nor are we given any arguments for his innocence or explanation for the barbarous cruelty of the Inquisitors. Poe's description of the pendulum blade's descent toward the narrator's heart is extremely graphic, but Poe uses the portrayal of explicit violence to create a suspenseful story rather than to condemn the Inquisition. The tale suggests a political agenda only implicitly. Poe does not critique the ideological basis of the tale's historical context. The narrative examines the physical and emotional fluctuations of the pure present, leaving historical and moral judgments to us. "The Pit and the Pendulum" is a traditional Poe story that breaks from Poe's conventions: violent yet ultimately hopeful, graphic yet politically allusive.

In the 1840 preface to *Tales of the Grotesque and Arabesque,* a collection of his short stories, Poe describes his authorial goal of "unity of design." In "The Philosophy of Composition," which was written three years after "The Pit and the Pendulum," he proclaims that the ideal short story must be short enough to be read at a single sitting. Moreover, he argues that all elements of a work of fiction should be crafted toward a single, intense effect. These critical theories merge in "The Pit and the Pendulum"; this short tale ruminates, at every moment, on the horror of its punishments without actually requiring that they be performed. Stripped of extraneous detail, the story focuses on what horror truly is: not the physical pain of death, but the terrible realization that a victim has no choice but to die. Whether the narrator chooses to jump into the pit or get sliced in half by the pendulum, he faces an identical outcome—death.

The horror of this lack of choice is the effect for which everything in the story strives. The story, however, holds out hope by demonstrating that true resolve when what someone chooses to do seems most impossible. When threatened by the pendulum, the narrator does not succumb to the swooning of his senses. He recruits his rational capacities and uses the hungry rats for his own benefit. In this way, the narrator resembles a character like C. Auguste Dupin in "The Murders in the Rue Morgue," who can separate himself from the emotional overload of a situation and put himself in a position to draw rational conclusions.

"THE BLACK CAT" (1843)

SUMMARY

On the eve of his death, an unnamed narrator opens the story by proclaiming that he is sane, despite the wild narrative he is about to convey. This narrative begins years before, when the narrator's honorable character is well known and celebrated. He confesses a great love for cats and dogs, both of which, he says, respect the fidelity of friendship, unlike fellow men. The narrator marries at a young age and introduces his wife to the domestic joys of owning pets. Among birds, goldfish, a dog, rabbits, and a monkey, the narrator singles out a large and beautiful black cat, named Pluto, as his favorite.

Though he loves Pluto, the narrator begins to suffer from violent mood swings, predominantly due to the influence of alcohol. He takes to mistreating not only the other animals but also his wife. During this uncontrollable rage, he spares only Pluto. After returning home quite drunk one night, the narrator lashes out at Pluto. Believing the cat has avoided him, he vengefully grasps the cat, only to be bitten on the hand. In demonic retaliation, the narrator pulls a penknife from his pocket and cuts out one of the cat's eyes. Though the narrator wakes the next morning with a partial feeling of remorse, he is unable to reverse the newly ominous course of his black soul. Ignored for certain now by the wounded cat, the narrator soon seeks further retaliation. He is overwhelmed by a spirit of PERVERSENESS, and sets out to commit wrong for the sake of wrong. He hangs Pluto from the limb of a tree one morning.

On the night of Pluto's hanging, the narrator's family's house burns down, but he dismisses the possibility of a connection between the two events. The day after the fire, which destroys all the narrator's possessions, he witnesses a group of neighbors collected around a wall that remains standing. Investigating their shouts of amazement, the narrator discovers the impression of a gigantic cat—with a rope around its neck—on the surface of the wall. The narrator attempts to explain rationally the existence of the impression, but he finds himself haunted by this phantasm over the course of many months. One night, while out drunk, the narrator discovers a black object poised upon a large barrel of alcohol. A new black cat has appeared, resembling Pluto but with a splash of white on his fur.

As with Pluto, the narrator experiences a great fondness for the mysterious cat, which no one has seen before. The cat becomes part of the household, much adored by his wife as well. However, following the earlier pattern, the narrator soon cannot resist feelings of hatred for the cat. These murderous sentiments intensify when the narrator discovers that the cat's splash of white fur has mysteriously taken on the shape of the gallows, the structure on which a hanging takes place. The white fur reveals the mode of execution that claimed Pluto, and the narrator pledges revenge.

One day, descending into the cellar of the building with his wife, the narrator almost trips over the cat. Enraged, the narrator grabs an axe to attack the cat, but his wife defends the animal. Further angered by this interference, the narrator turns his rage at his wife and buries the axe in her head. Faced with the evidence of his crime, the narrator considers many options for the body's disposal, including dismemberment and burial. The narrator eventually decides to take advantage of the damp walls in the basement and entomb the body behind their plaster. Without any difficulty, the narrator creates a tomb in the plaster wall, thereby hiding the body and all traces of his murder. When he finally turns to the cat, it is missing, and he concludes that it has been frightened away by his anger.

On the fourth day after the murder, the police arrive unexpectedly at the narrator's apartment. Cool and collected, the narrator leads them through the premises, even into the basement. Though facing the scene of the crime, the police do not demonstrate any curiosity and prepare to leave the residence. The narrator, however, keeps trying to allay their suspicion. Commenting upon the solid craftsmanship of the house, he taps on the wall—behind which is his wife's body—with a cane. In response to the tapping, a long, loud cry emanates from behind the wall. The police storm the wall and dismantle it, discovering the hidden corpse. Upon its head sits the missing cat.

Analysis

Much like "The Tell-Tale Heart," "The Black Cat" follows the narrator's descent into madness after he proclaims his sanity in the tale's opening paragraph. Even the narrator acknowledges the "wild" nature of the tale, attempting thereby to separate his mental condition from the events of the plot. The nature of the narrator's madness differs from that of the narrator of "The Tell-Tale Heart." "The Black Cat" does not concern itself only with the self-contained nature of the narrator's mind. Rather, the narrator confesses an alcoholism that interferes with his grasp on reality and produces mood swings. Alcohol is, like the cat, an external agent that intrudes on the dynamics of the plot. The introduction of alcohol as a plot device is also significant because Edgar Allan Poe was an reputedly uncontrollable drunk throughout his lifetime. For many years, his biographers asserted that he died of alcohol poisoning in a gutter in Baltimore. More recent biographies insist that the exact cause of Poe's death cannot be determined. Regardless, it is certain that Poe suffered from the deleterious effects of alcohol consumption throughout his life.

The influential literary critic Tzvetan Todorov introduced a concept of the "fantastic" in the early 1970s to discuss literature of horror, and the idea can be applied usefully to "The Black Cat." The fantastic, he asserts, explores the indefinite boundary between the real and the supernatural. The fantastic is a literary category that contains elements of both the rational and the irrational. One of the fantastic elements in "The Black Cat" is the existence of the second cat—with the changing shape of its white fur and its appearance on the corpse behind the wall. These plot twists challenge reality, but they do not completely substitute a supernatural explanation for a logical one. It is possible that the plot twists derive only from the insanity of the narrator. As a result, the plot twists, like the fantastic, hover between the real and the supernatural. The resolution of the story is both rationally possible and tremendously unlikely; the cat could inhabit the basement walls, but it is difficult to believe that it would remain silently in the wall for a long time or go unnoticed by the overly meticulous narrator.

"THE PURLOINED LETTER" (1844)

SUMMARY

In a small room in Paris, an unnamed narrator, who also narrates "The Murders in the Rue Morgue," sits quietly with his friend, C. Auguste Dupin. He ponders the murders in the Rue Morgue, which Dupin solved in that story. Monsieur G——, the prefect of the Paris police, arrives, having decided to consult Dupin again. The prefect presents a case that is almost too simple: a letter has been taken from the royal apartments. The police know who has taken it: the Minister D——, an important government official. According to the prefect, a young lady possessed the letter, which contains information that could harm a powerful individual. When the young lady was first reading the letter, the man whom it concerned came into the royal apartments. Not wanting to arouse his suspicion, she put it down on a table next to her. The sinister Minister D—— then walked in and noted the letter's contents. Quickly grasping the seriousness of the situation, he produced a letter of his own that resembled the important letter. He left his own letter next to the original one as he began to talk of Parisian affairs. Finally, as he prepared to leave the apartment, he purposely retrieved the lady's letter in place of his own. Now, the prefect explains, the Minister D—— possesses a great deal of power over the lady.

Dupin asks whether the police have searched the Minister's residence, arguing that since the power of the letter derives from its being readily available, it must be in his apartment. The prefect responds that they have searched the Minister's residence but have not located the letter. He recounts the search procedure, during which the police systematically searched every inch of the hotel. In addition, the letter could not be hidden on the Minister's body because the police have searched him as well. The prefect mentions that he is willing to search long and hard because the reward offered in the case is so generous. Upon Dupin's request, the prefect reads him a physical description of the letter. Dupin suggests that the police search again.

One month later, Dupin and the narrator are again sitting together when the prefect visits. The prefect admits that he cannot find the letter, even though the reward has increased. The prefect says that he will pay 50,000 francs to anyone who obtains the letter for him. Dupin tells him to write a check for that amount on the spot. Upon receipt of the check, Dupin hands over the letter. The prefect rushes off to return it to its rightful owner, and Dupin explains how he obtained the letter.

Dupin admits that the police are skilled investigators according to their own principles. He explains this remark by describing a young boy playing "even and odd." In this game, each player must guess whether the number of things (usually toys) held by another player is even or odd. If the guesser is right, he gets one of the toys. If he is wrong, he loses a toy of his own. The boy whom Dupin describes plays the game well because he bases his guesses on the knowledge of his opponent. When he faces difficulty, he imitates the facial expression of his opponent, as though to understand what he thinks and feels. With this knowledge, he often guesses correctly.

Dupin argues that the Paris police do not use this strategy and therefore could not find the letter: the police think only to look for a letter in places where they themselves might hide it.

Dupin argues that the Minister D—— is intelligent enough not to hide the letter in the nooks and crannies of his apartment—exactly where the police first investigate. He describes to the narrator a game of puzzles in which one player finds a name on a map and tells the other player to find it as well. Amateurs, says Dupin, pick the names with the smallest letters. According to Dupin's logic, the hardest names to find are actually those that stretch broadly across the map because they are so obvious.

With this game in mind, Dupin recounts the visit he made to the Minister's apartment. After surveying the Minister's residence, Dupin notices a group of visiting cards hanging from the mantelpiece. A letter accompanies them. It has a different exterior than that previously described by the prefect, but Dupin also observes that the letter appears to have been folded back on itself. He becomes sure that it is the stolen document. In order to create a reason for returning to the apartment, he purposely leaves behind his snuffbox. When he goes back the next morning to retrieve it, he also arranges for someone to make a commotion outside the window while he is in the apartment. When the Minister rushes to the window to investigate the noise, Dupin replaces the stolen letter with a fake. He justifies his decision to leave behind another letter by predicting that the Minister will embarrass himself when he acts in reliance upon the letter he falsely believes he still possesses. Dupin remarks that the Minister once wronged him in Vienna and that he has pledged not to forget the insult. Inside the fake letter, then, Dupin inscribes, a French poem that translates into English, "So baneful a scheme, if not worthy of Atreus, is worthy of Thyestes."

ANALYSIS

Along with "The Murders in the Rue Morgue," "The Purloined Letter" establishes a new genre of short fiction in American literature: the detective story. Poe considered "The Purloined Letter" his best detective story, and critics have long identified the ways in which it redefines the mystery genre—it turns away from action toward intellectual analysis, for example. As opposed to the graphic violence of "The Murders in the Rue Morgue," which features bodily mutilation and near decapitation by a wild animal, "The Purloined Letter" focuses more dryly on the relationship between the Paris police and Dupin, between the ineffectual established order and the savvy private eye. When the narrator opens the story by reflecting upon the gruesome murders in the Rue Morgue that Dupin has helped to solve, Poe makes it clear that the prior story is on his mind. Poe sets up the cool reason of "The Purloined Letter" in opposition to the violence of "The Murders in the Rue Morgue." The battered and lacerated bodies of "The Murders in the Rue Morgue" are replaced by the bloodless, inanimate stolen letter. However, just as the Paris police are unable to solve the gory crime of passion in "The Murders in the Rue Morgue," they are similarly unable to solve this apparently simple mystery, in which the solution is hidden in plain sight.

Poe moves away from violence and action by associating Dupin's intelligence with his reflectiveness and his radical theories about the mind. This tale does not have the constant action of stories like "The Cask of Amontillado" or "The Black Cat." Instead, this tale features the narrator and Dupin sitting in Dupin's library and discussing ideas. The tale's action, relayed by flashbacks, takes place outside the narrative frame. The narrative itself is told through dispassionate analysis. The intrusions of the prefect and his investigations of the Minister's apartment come off as unrefined and unintellectual. Poe portrays the prefect as simultaneously the most active and the most unreflective character in the story. Dupin's most pointed criticisms of the prefect have less to do with a personal attack than with a critique of the mode of investigation employed by the police as a whole. Dupin suggests that the police cannot think outside their own standard procedures. They are unable to place themselves in the minds of those who actually commit crimes. Dupin's strategy of solving crimes, on the other hand, involves a process of thinking like someone else. Just as the boy playing "even and odd" enters his opponent's mind, Dupin inhabits the consciousness of the criminal. He does not employ fancy psychological theories, but rather imitates the train of thought of his opponent. He succeeds in operating one step ahead of the police because he thinks as the Minister does.

This crime-solving technique of thinking like the criminal suggests that Dupin and the Minister are more doubles than opposites. The revenge aspect of the story, which Dupin promises after the Minister offends him in Vienna, arguably derives from their threatening similarity. Dupin's note inside the phony letter, translated "So baneful a scheme, if not worthy of Atreus, is worthy of Thyestes," suggests the rivalry that accompanies brotherly minds.

In the French dramatist Crébillon's early-eighteenth-century tragedy *Atrée et Thyeste* (or *Atreus and Thyestes*), Thyestes seduces
the wife of his brother, Atreus. In retaliation, Atreus murders the
sons of Thyestes and serves them to their father at a feast. Dupin
implies here that Thyestes deserves more punishment than Atreus
because he commits the original wrong. In contrast, Atreus's
revenge is legitimate because it repays the original offense. Dupin
considers his own deed to be revenge and thereby morally justified.

"THE MASQUE OF THE RED DEATH" (1845)

SUMMARY

A disease known as the Red Death plagues the fictional country
where this tale is set, and it causes its victims to die quickly and grue-
somely. Even though this disease is spreading rampantly, the prince,
Prospero, feels happy and hopeful. He decides to lock the gates of
his palace in order to fend off the plague, ignoring the illness ravag-
ing the land. After several months, he throws a fancy masquerade
ball. For this celebration, he decorates the rooms of his house in single colors. The easternmost room is decorated in blue, with blue
stained-glass windows. The next room is purple with the same
stained-glass window pattern. The rooms continue westward,
according to this design, in the following color arrangement: green,
orange, white, and violet. The seventh room is black, with red windows. Also in this room stands an ebony clock. When the clock rings
each hour, its sound is so loud and distracting that everyone stops
talking and the orchestra stops playing. When the clock is not
sounding, though, the rooms are so beautiful and strange that they
seem to be filled with dreams, swirling among the revelers. Most
guests, however, avoid the final, black-and-red room because it contains both the clock and an ominous ambience.

At midnight, a new guest appears, dressed more ghoulishly than
his counterparts. His mask looks like the face of a corpse, his gar-
ments resemble a funeral shroud, and his face reveals spots of blood
suggesting that he is a victim of the Red Death. Prospero becomes
angry that someone with so little humor and levity would join his
party. The other guests, however, are so afraid of this masked man
that they fail to prevent him from walking through each room. Prospero finally catches up to the new guest in the black-and-red room.

As soon as he confronts the figure, Prospero dies. When other party-goers enter the room to attack the cloaked man, they find that there is nobody beneath the costume. Everyone then dies, for the Red Death has infiltrated the castle. "Darkness and Decay and the Red Death" have at last triumphed.

ANALYSIS

"The Masque of the Red Death" is an allegory. It features a set of recognizable symbols whose meanings combine to convey a message. An allegory always operates on two levels of meaning: the literal elements of the plot (the colors of the rooms, for example) and their symbolic counterparts, which often involve large philosophical concepts (such as life and death). We can read this story as an allegory about life and death and the powerlessness of humans to evade the grip of death. The Red Death thus represents, both literally and allegorically, death. No matter how beautiful the castle, how luxuriant the clothing, or how rich the food, no mortal, not even a prince, can escape death. In another sense, though, the story also means to punish Prospero's arrogant belief that he can use his wealth to fend off the natural, tragic progress of life. Prospero's arrogance combines with a grievous insensitivity to the plight of his less fortunate countrymen. Although he possesses the wealth to assist those in need, he turns his wealth into a mode of self-defense and decadent self-indulgence. His decadence in throwing the masquerade ball, however, unwittingly positions him as a caged animal, with no possible escape.

The rooms of the palace, lined up in a series, allegorically represent the stages of life. Poe makes it a point to arrange the rooms running from east to west. This progression is symbolically significant because it represents the life cycle of a day: the sun rises in the east and sets in the west, with night symbolizing death. What transforms this set of symbols into an allegory, however, is the further symbolic treatment of the twenty-four hour life cycle: it translates to the realm of human beings. This progression from east to west, performed by both Prospero and the mysterious guest, symbolizes the human journey from birth to death. Poe crafts the last, black room as the ominous endpoint, the room the guests fear just as they fear death. The clock that presides over that room also reminds the guests of death's final judgment. The hourly ringing of the bells is a reminder of the passing of time, inexorable and ultimately personal.

As in many Poe stories, the use of names contributes to the symbolic economic context of the story and suggests another set of allegorical interpretations. For example, Prospero, whose name suggests financial prosperity, exploits his own wealth to stave off the infiltration of the Red Death. His retreat to the protection of an aristocratic palace may also allegorize a type of economic system that Poe suggests is doomed to failure. In the hierarchical relationship between Prospero and the peasantry, Poe portrays the unfairness of a feudal system, where wealth lies in the hands of the aristocracy while the peasantry suffers. This use of feudal imagery is historically accurate, in that feudalism was prevalent when the actual Bubonic Plague devastated Europe in the fourteenth century. The Red Death, then, embodies a type of radical egalitarianism, or monetary equality, because it attacks the rich and poor alike.

The portrayal of the masquerade ball foreshadows the similar setting of the carnival in "The Cask of Amontillado," which appeared less than a year after "The Masque of the Red Death." Whereas the carnival in "The Cask of Amontillado" associates drunken revelry with an open-air Italian celebration, the masquerade functions in this story as a celebratory retreat from the air itself, which has become infected by the plague. The masquerade, however, dispels the sense of claustrophobia within the palace by liberating the inner demons of the guests. These demons are then embodied by the grotesque costumes. Like the carnival, the masquerade urges the abandonment of social conventions and rigid senses of personal identity. However, the mysterious guest illuminates the extent to which Prospero and his guests police the limits of social convention. When the mysterious guest uses his costume to portray the fears that the masquerade is designed to counteract, Prospero responds antagonistically. As he knows, the prosperity of the party relies upon the psychological transformation of fear about the Red Death into revelry. When the mysterious guest dramatizes his own version of revelry as the fear that cannot be spoken, he violates an implicit social rule of the masquerade. The fall of Prospero and the subsequent deaths of his guests follow from this logic of the masquerade: when revelry is unmasked as a defense mechanism against fear, then the raw exposure of what lies beneath is enough to kill.

"THE CASK OF AMONTILLADO" (1846)

"For the love of God, Montresor!"
(See QUOTATIONS, p. 61)

SUMMARY

The narrator, Montresor, opens the story by stating that he has been irreparably insulted by his acquaintance, Fortunato, and that he seeks revenge. He wants to exact this revenge, however, in a measured way, without placing himself at risk. He decides to use Fortunato's fondness for wine against him. During the carnival season, Montresor, wearing a mask of black silk, approaches Fortunato. He tells Fortunato that he has acquired something that could pass for Amontillado, a light Spanish sherry. Fortunato (Italian for "fortunate") wears the multicolored costume of the jester, including a cone cap with bells. Montresor tells Fortunato that if he is too busy, he will ask a man named Luchesi to taste it. Fortunato apparently considers Luchesi a competitor and claims that this man could not tell Amontillado from other types of sherry. Fortunato is anxious to taste the wine and to determine for Montresor whether or not it is truly Amontillado. Fortunato insists that they go to Montresor's vaults.

Montresor has strategically planned for this meeting by sending his servants away to the carnival. The two men descend into the damp vaults, which are covered with nitre, or saltpeter, a whitish mineral. Apparently aggravated by the nitre, Fortunato begins to cough. The narrator keeps offering to bring Fortunato back home, but Fortunato refuses. Instead, he accepts wine as the antidote to his cough. The men continue to explore the deep vaults, which are full of the dead bodies of the Montresor family. In response to the crypts, Fortunato claims to have forgotten Montresor's family coat of arms and motto. Montresor responds that his family shield portrays "a huge human foot d'or, in a field azure; the foot crushes a serpent rampant whose fangs are imbedded in the heel." The motto, in Latin, is "nemo me impune lacessit," that is, "no one attacks me with impunity."

Later in their journey, Fortunato makes a hand movement that is a secret sign of the Masons, an exclusive fraternal organization. Montresor does not recognize this hand signal, though he claims that he is a Mason. When Fortunato asks for proof, Montresor shows him his trowel, the implication being that Montresor is an actual stonemason. Fortunato says that he must be jesting, and the two men continue onward. The men walk into a crypt, where human bones decorate three of the four walls. The bones from the fourth wall have been thrown down on the ground. On the exposed wall is a small recess, where Montresor tells Fortunato that the Amontillado is being stored. Fortunato, now heavily intoxicated, goes to the back of the recess. Montresor then suddenly chains the slow-footed Fortunato to a stone.

Taunting Fortunato with an offer to leave, Montresor begins to wall up the entrance to this small crypt, thereby trapping Fortunato inside. Fortunato screams confusedly as Montresor builds the first layer of the wall. The alcohol soon wears off and Fortunato moans, terrified and helpless. As the layers continue to rise, though, Fortunato falls silent. Just as Montresor is about to finish, Fortunato laughs as if Montresor is playing a joke on him, but Montresor is not joking. At last, after a final plea, "For the love of God, Montresor!" Fortunato stops answering Montresor, who then twice calls out his enemy's name. After no response, Montresor claims that his heart feels sick because of the dampness of the catacombs. He fits the last stone into place and plasters the wall closed, his actions accompanied only by the jingling of Fortunato's bells. He finally repositions the bones on the fourth wall. For fifty years, he writes, no one has disturbed them. He concludes with a Latin phrase meaning "May he rest in peace."

ANALYSIS

The terror of "The Cask of Amontillado," as in many of Poe's tales, resides in the lack of evidence that accompanies Montresor's claims to Fortunato's "thousand injuries" and "insult." The story features revenge and secret murder as a way to avoid using legal channels for retribution. Law is nowhere on Montresor's—or Poe's—radar screen, and the enduring horror of the story is the fact of punishment without proof. Montresor uses his subjective experience of Fortunato's insult to name himself judge, jury, and executioner in this tale, which also makes him an unreliable narrator. Montresor confesses this story fifty years after its occurrence; such a significant passage of time between the events and the narration of the events makes the narrative all the more unreliable. Montresor's unreliability overrides the rational consideration of evidence, such as particular occurrences of insult, that would necessarily precede any guilty sentence in a non-Poe world. "The Cask of Amontillado" takes subjective interpretation—the fact that different people interpret the same things differently—to its horrific endpoint.

Poe's use of color imagery is central to his questioning of Montresor's motives. His face covered in a black silk mask, Montresor represents not blind justice but rather its Gothic opposite: biased revenge. In contrast, Fortunato dons the motley-colored costume of the court fool, who gets literally and tragically fooled by Montresor's masked motives. The color schemes here represent the irony of Fortunato's death sentence. Fortunato, Italian for "the fortunate one," faces the realization that even the carnival season can be murderously serious. Montresor chooses the setting of the carnival for its abandonment of social order. While the carnival usually indicates joyful social interaction, Montresor distorts its merry abandon, turning the carnival on its head. The repeated allusions to the bones of Montresor's family that line the vaults foreshadow the story's descent into the underworld. The two men's underground travels are a metaphor for their trip to hell. Because the carnival, in the land of the living, does not occur as Montresor wants it to, he takes the carnival below ground, to the realm of the dead and the satanic.

To build suspense in the story, Poe often employs foreshadowing. For example, when Fortunato says, "I shall not die of a cough," Montresor replies, "True," because he knows that Fortunato will in fact die from dehydration and starvation in the crypt. Montresor's description of his family's coat of arms also foreshadows future events. The shield features a human foot crushing a tenacious serpent. In this image, the foot represents Montresor and the serpent represents Fortunato. Although Fortunato has hurt Montresor with biting insults, Montresor will ultimately crush him. The conversation about Masons also foreshadows Fortunato's demise. Fortunato challenges Montresor's claim that he is a member of the Masonic order, and Montresor replies insidiously with a visual pun. When he declares that he is a "mason" by showing his trowel, he means that he is a literal stonemason—that is, that he constructs things out of stones and mortar, namely Fortunato's grave.

The final moments of conversation between Montresor and Fortunato heighten the horror and suggest that Fortunato ultimately—and ironically—achieves some type of upper hand over Montresor. Fortunato's plea, "For the love of God, Montresor!" has provoked much critical controversy. Some critics suggest that Montresor has at last brought Fortunato to the pit of desperation and despair, indicated by his invocation of a God that has long left him behind. Other critics, however, argue that Fortunato ultimately mocks the "love of God," thereby employing the same irony that Montresor has effectively used to lure him to the crypts. These are Fortunato's final words, and the strange desperation that Montresor demonstrates in response suggests that he needs Fortunato more than he wants to admit. Only when he twice screams "Fortunato!" loudly, with no response, does Montresor claim to have a sick heart. The reasons for Fortunato's silence are unclear, but perhaps his willing refusal to answer Montresor is a type of strange victory in otherwise dire circumstances.

IMPORTANT QUOTATIONS EXPLAINED

1.   "For the love of God, Montresor!"

In "The Cask of Amontillado," Fortunato addresses this plea—his last spoken words—to Montresor, the man who has entombed him alive. Critics have long argued about the meaning of this quotation. On the one hand, some argue that Fortunato at last breaks down and, realizing the deathly import of the situation, resorts to a prayer for earthly salvation. Fortunato, according to this interpretation, maintains the hope that Montresor is playing a complex practical joke. The italicized words signal the panic in Fortunato's voice as he tries to redeem Montresor from the grip of evil. On the other hand, some critics assert that Fortunato accepts his earthly demise and instead mocks the capacity for prayer to influence life on Earth. In this interpretation, Fortunato recognizes his own misfortune and taunts Montresor with the mention of a God who has long ago deserted him. Just as the carnival represents the liberation from respectable social behavior in the streets above, the crypts below dramatize religious abandon and the violation of sacred humanity.

Montresor's response of "Yes, for the love of God!" mocks Fortunato in his moment of desperate vulnerability. However, Fortunato refuses to acknowledge this final insult. On the verge of death, he uses silence as his final weapon. He recognizes that his unknowing participation in the entombment has given Montresor more satisfaction than the murder itself. When Montresor twice calls out "Fortunato!" he hears only the jingle of Fortunato's cap bells in response. The sense of panic shifts here from Fortunato to Montresor. Montresor's heart grows sick as he realizes that Fortunato outwits him by refusing to play along anymore in this game of revenge. Montresor faces only the physical fact of the murder, and is stripped of the psychological satisfaction of having fooled Fortunato.

2. "In me didst thou exist—and, in my death, see by this image, which is thine own, how utterly thou hast murdered thyself."

In "William Wilson," the rivalrous double William Wilson utters these final words to the narrator, the man who has just stabbed him. This quotation, spoken with reference to an image in a mirror, points to the indistinguishability between the victim, William Wilson, and the narrator, William Wilson. The speaker uses the image of the mirror to represent his own death, but the mirror eerily reflects the image of the narrator, not the speaker. The quotation highlights the inseparability of the self and the rivalrous double, for the murder of the rival also produces the suicide of the self. The second William Wilson constitutes the narrator's alter ego, the part of his own being that he has externalized in the figure of his competitor. Although the narrator believes he can use violence to curtail the power of his alter ego, he discovers that he owes his life to the person he most despises.

This quotation also points to the fine line between love and hate. The second William Wilson's final words are not bitter or vengeful. Their compassionate insight precisely contrasts with the narrator's act of violence that has triggered the quotation. William Wilson uses these words not only to convey his intimate knowledge about the narrator, but also to redeem the narrator from the paranoia that has taken his life. The quotation discloses the rivals' indistinguishability so that the narrator might recognize that his own mental pathology has killed him. Whereas the narrator has construed their similarity as grounds for jealousy and violence, his rival alternatively uses their doubling to convey difficult, and potentially redemptive, knowledge to the narrator. In this way, William Wilson, until his final breath, plays right into the narrator's jealousy by rejecting the very lust for vengeance that the narrator has been unable to escape. In the end, the narrator's suicide proves a tragic alternative to William Wilson's compassionate self-knowledge.

3.   "In investigations such as we are now pursuing, it
      should not be so much asked 'what has occurred,' as
      'what has occurred that has never occurred before.'"

In "The Murders in the Rue Morgue," Parisian private detective M. Auguste Dupin speaks these words to the narrator as the two men begin to inspect the gruesome crime scene. Dupin here sets out to explain his analytic approach to solving crimes. He accuses the Paris police of being too shortsighted in their investigative strategies by limiting their interest to "what has occurred." By Dupin's logic, the police fail to solve the murders in the Rue Morgue because the crimes move beyond the range of both their experience and their imagination. Instead of pooling their imaginative resources, the Paris police get distracted by the crime's gruesome elements. According to Dupin, while the best police minds can be, at times, ingenious, they often fail to be adequately creative.

Dupin distinguishes himself from the established police order in two ways. First, he approaches the ghastly violence of the scene dispassionately, treating it as a mathematical study. He is thus able to avoid becoming overwhelmed by the scene's emotional trauma. Second, Dupin expands the methodological reach of crime-solving by relying upon intuition and analysis. Not only does Dupin gather evidence from the crime scene that has previously escaped the notice of the police, like the window nails, but he is also able to adequately account for details that confuse others. For example, he translates the medical examiner's report of the immense, almost superhuman strength of the murderer into the possibility of a nonhuman having committed the crime. Dupin's effectiveness lies in his eccentric willingness to move beyond certain standards of rationality and believability. While his explanations piece together the disparate clues from the crime scene in an eminently rational way, he begins with premises that seem irrational—for example, that an animal could have committed the crime. Dupin utilizes such controversial premises because they privilege new modes of analysis—that is, consideration of what "has never occurred before."

4.   I cannot, for my soul, remember how, when, or even
      precisely where, I first became acquainted with the
      lady Ligeia.

The narrator opens "Ligeia" by confessing certain gaps in his memory of his beloved first wife. The narrator's scant memory contrasts
with the plot of the tale itself, which ultimately portrays Ligeia as
one of Poe's most enduring revenants, or women who return from
the grave. While the narrator claims to have forgotten the specific
circumstances in which he met Ligeia, the tale proceeds to establish
Ligeia as an unforgettable presence. When the lady Rowena, the
narrator's second wife, becomes mysteriously ill in the second
month of their marriage, the narrator has to fend off his memories
of Ligeia. The tale affirms Ligeia's power in contrast to the narrator's claims of feeble memory. It thereby distinguishes "Ligeia" from
Poe's other first-person Gothic narrations by shifting attention from
the narrator's unreliability to the motif of the woman who return
from the dead. While the plot highlights the irony of the narrator's
opening words, Poe does not make the narrator's contradictions the
centerpiece of the narrative's interest.

     Ligeia's obscure origins, as portrayed in this quotation, contrib-
ute to her Gothic status as a revenant. She possesses a certain Gothic
allure because she seems to come from nowhere and to be free from
the laws of nature that govern both the narrator and Rowena.
Ligeia's mysterious return in the tale's final scene effectively reenacts
the narrator's opening remark about her sudden and mysterious
appearance in his life. In this sense, while the tale undermines the
narrator's claims of feeble memory, his initial remark also foreshadows Ligeia's Gothic return. She comes from nowhere in the tale's
eerie conclusion just as she originally presents herself to the narrator
as his beloved wife without a past.

5. A striking similitude between the brother and the sister now first arrested my attention; and Usher, divining, perhaps, my thoughts, murmured out some few words from which I learned that the deceased and himself had been twins, and that sympathies of a scarcely intelligible nature had always existed between them.

In "The Fall of the House of Usher," the narrator makes this observation about Roderick and Madeline Usher when he helps to bury Madeline after her apparent death. This quotation makes explicit the motif of the doppelganger, or character double, that characterizes the relationship between Roderick and Madeline. Poe philosophically experiments with a split between mind and body by associating Roderick exclusively with the former and Madeline exclusively with the latter. The doppelganger motif undermines the separation between mind and body. Poe represents this intimate connectivity between mind and body by making Roderick and Madeline biological twins. When sickness afflicts one sibling, for example, it contagiously spreads to the other. The mode of contagion implies an early version of ESP, or extrasensory perception. Poe insinuates that these mysterious sympathies, which move beyond biological definition, also possess the capacity to transmit physical illness. It is also possible to view these sympathies as Poe's avant-garde imagining of genetic transmission between siblings.

Poe suggests that the twin relationship involves not only physical similitude but also psychological or supernatural communication. The power of the intimate relationship between the twins pervades the incestuous framework of the Usher line, since the mansion contains all surviving branches of the family. The revelation of this intimacy also reaffirms the narrator's status as an outsider. The narrator realizes that Roderick and Madeline are twins only after she is nearly dead, and this ignorance embodies the fact that the walls of the Usher mansion have protected the family from outsiders up to the point of the narrator's arrival. When the narrator, as an outsider, discovers the similitude between Roderick and Madeline, he begins to invade a privileged space of family knowledge that ultimately falls to ruins in the presence of a trespasser.

QUOTATIONS

Key Facts

FULL TITLE
"MS. Found in a Bottle" (1833); "Ligeia" (1838); "The Fall of the House of Usher" (1839); "William Wilson" (1839); "The Murders in the Rue Morgue" (1841); "The Tell-Tale Heart" (1843); "The Pit and the Pendulum" (1843); "The Black Cat" (1843); "The Purloined Letter" (1844); "The Masque of the Red Death" (1845); "The Cask of Amontillado" (1846)

AUTHOR
Edgar Allan Poe

TYPE OF WORK
Short story

GENRE
Gothic short story; detective story; science fiction

LANGUAGE
English

TIME AND PLACE WRITTEN
1830–1846; Baltimore, Richmond, Philadelphia, New York

PUBLISHER
Saturday Visiter (Baltimore); *Southern Literary Messenger* (Richmond); *Burton's Gentleman's Magazine* (Philadelphia); *Graham's* (Philadelphia); *Evening Mirror* (New York)

NARRATOR
In the tales of criminal insanity, Poe's narrators are unnamed and often unreliable. They claim their sanity and then proceed to detail their pathological madness. In the detective stories, the narrator is a loyal friend of Dupin and is in awe of the crime solver's brilliance.

POINT OF VIEW
In the tales of criminal insanity, Poe's first-person narrators produce unreliable confessions. They control the narrative, and we see only through their eyes. However, they describe their own pathological actions so meticulously that they demonstrate that they are actually insane. They are unable to step back from

their narratives to discern their own madness. In the detective stories, Poe employs a third-person narrator, a friend of Dupin, and while the narrator tries to convey the tale fairly, his loyalty to Dupin prevents him from questioning or doubting Dupin's actions and strategies.

TONE

In the tales of criminal insanity, the narrators' diction, which is precise and often ornate, suggests a serious investment in confession as a defense of sanity. In the detective stories, Poe's narrator attempts a dispassionate and fair account of the events, but he often humbly defers to Dupin at moments of confusion or complexity.

TENSE

The tales of criminal insanity often begin in the present tense as confessions and then flash back to recount past crimes. The detective stories also feature little action in the present and instead convey the important events as flashbacks.

PROTAGONIST

The tales of criminal insanity establish the first-person narrators as protagonists by focusing on their struggles with madness and the law. The detective stories feature Dupin as the protagonist by focusing on his ability to save the Paris police with crime-solving brilliance.

THEMES

The similarity of love and hate; the rivalry between self and alter ego; the personification of memory after death

MOTIFS

The revenant; the doppelganger; the masquerade

SYMBOLS

Eyes; the whirlpool; "Fortunato"

Study Questions & Essay Topics

Study Questions

1. *How does Poe portray the motif of the doppelganger, or character double, in his two tales of 1839, "The Fall of the House of Usher" and "William Wilson"?*

Though Poe examines the doppelganger in both "The Fall of the House of Usher" and "William Wilson," he emphasizes different aspects of its character in the two stories. For example, in "The Fall of the House of Usher," Poe presents the possibility of a complete split between mind and body in the twin siblings of Roderick and Madeline. The siblings are an external representation of the philosophical relationship between mind and body, but become overly identified with their respective halves of the equation. Insofar as sickness plagues both siblings, Poe suggests that a complete split between mind and body is ultimately impossible.

In "William Wilson," Poe is less interested in the external agents of mind and body than in their internalized effects. The narrator's alter ego, in fact, embodies a figment of the narrator's own paranoid imagination. The narrator creates a physical doppelganger out of his own mental pathology. When the narrator attempts to resolve this rivalry with the plunge of a sword, Poe demonstrates, as in "The Fall of the House of Usher," the bodily effects of mental disease. However, the narrator's attempt to murder his foe is actually an act of suicide, as his hated competitor represents a part of his own being. If Roderick and Madeline represent the external components of the mind-body split, then "William Wilson" condenses these two components into one body haunted by a split personality.

QUESTIONS & ESSAYS

2. *In "The Tell-Tale Heart" and "The Black Cat," what is the
    relationship between the confessions of Poe's guilty
    narrators and their claims to sanity and reliability?*

Although they are guilty, Poe's narrators in these tales experience an
irresistible urge to confess to their crimes. While each explains the
circumstances of his hideous actions, he also attempts to defend his
sanity. Each provides a rational explanation of his mental fixations
and portrays his criminal activity as excusable within the logic of his
confessions. These two narrators use the form of the confession to
explain away the content of their actions, but Poe uses this intimate
connection between form and content to undermine their reliability
as narrators.

In "The Tell-Tale Heart," for example, the narrator masters the
form of the confession in order to defend against charges of insanity.
He believes that a precise description of his murder of the old man
will establish his reliability as a sane narrator. In other words, he
trusts in the intimate connection between form and content, but he
never understands that the murderous content of his confession can
make the clearness of his form irrelevant. He is unable to perceive
that by admitting his irrational fixation on a vulture-eye, he reveals
his own mental pathology.

Similarly, in "The Black Cat," the narrator defends the reliability
of his narrative but cannot fully explain his transition to cruelty. On
the one hand, he offers the external substance of alcohol as a rational explanation for his mood swings and his hanging of Pluto. On
the other hand, though, he then uncritically accepts the appearance
of the second cat with its changing fur in the shape of the gallows.
The narrator unwittingly portrays his own insanity by demonstrating his inability to escape the hauntings of the second cat. Poe suggests that the second cat is, in part, the projection of the narrator's
guilty conscience, and the story ultimately undermines any faith in
the narrator's descriptions of the reincarnated cat. Though he
employs the form of the confession to explain his actions, the narrator fails to see that these actions illustrate his deranged mentality.

3. *How does Poe use setting as a Gothic element in "The Pit and the Pendulum," "The Cask of Amontillado," and "The Masque of the Red Death"?*

Poe elicits terror in these stories by enclosing his characters within confined settings that take on Gothic characteristics. For example, the title "The Pit and the Pendulum" indicates the degree to which Poe invests the setting of the story with the capacity for terror. The setting, a prison cell, becomes a metaphor for the authoritarian power of the Inquisition. We never see any human representatives of the Inquisition. Rather, the physical features of the setting—the pit, the pendulum, and the rats—become substitutes for the cruelty and the violence of the Inquisition's human leaders. In this way, Poe imbues the physical setting with the human capacity for evil.

In "The Cask of Amontillado," setting becomes an instrument of revenge and murder. While the human perpetrators of the Inquisition remain elusive in "The Pit and the Pendulum," Montresor functions here as the criminal mastermind who orchestrates the transformation of his family's crypts into a crime scene. Though the crypts already invoke imagery of death even before Fortunato's demise, Montresor modifies their function. He uses them to kill, rather than merely to contain the bodies of those already dead. Montresor transforms a hallowed family space of memory and tribute into a weapon of revenge. His murder of Fortunato contains, in this way, an element of irony, as the crypts unwittingly make Fortunato a symbolic member of Montresor's family and past.

"The Masque of the Red Death" uses the palace setting as part of its allegorical statement about the inevitability of death. Whereas Prince Prospero believes he can use the walls of his palace to fend off the spread of the Red Death, the story reveals that death knows no boundaries. The lavish setting of the palace on the night of the masquerade also contrasts with the impoverished living conditions of the surrounding peasants, who are the first to suffer from the plague. The interior layout of the palace, which promotes the progression of guests from east to west, is an allegory for the life cycle of a day. With the westernmost room, which features the color black and contains a massive clock, Poe suggests that all the guests must end up in this room of death, which ticks away the hours of life.

SUGGESTED ESSAY TOPICS

1.   How does Poe use black and white color imagery in "MS. Found in a Bottle" and "Ligeia"? How might this use of black and white imagery relate to tensions about slavery in the mid-nineteenth century?

2.   How does Poe portray family in "The Fall of the House of Usher" and "The Cask of Amontillado"?

3.   How does Dupin demonstrate his mathematical mind in "The Murders in the Rue Morgue" and "The Purloined Letter"? How does Dupin's analytical mind compare to the scientific imagination of the narrator from "MS. Found in a Bottle"?

4.   Why does Poe have Dupin attempt to solve such drastically different crimes in "The Murders in the Rue Morgue" and "The Purloined Letter"?

5.   What is the role of history in "The Pit and the Pendulum"? How does the specificity of the tale's historical placement contribute to its aura of terror?

6.   Is the narrator of "William Wilson" insane? Compare and contrast him with the narrator of "The Tell-Tale Heart."

Review & Resources

Quiz

1. How many rooms does Prince Prospero's palace contain?

   A. Five
   B. Three
   C. Ten
   D. Seven

2. With which river does the narrator of "Ligeia" associate his first wife?

   A. The Seine
   B. The Rhine
   C. The Mississippi
   D. The Po

3. Who is the author of "Mad Trist," the romance that the narrator reads to Roderick Usher?

   A. Sir Launcelot Canning
   B. Geoffrey of Monmouth
   C. Geoffrey Chaucer
   D. The Venerable Bede

4. In "The Black Cat," what is the name of the narrator's first cat?

   A. Saturn
   B. Pluto
   C. Mercury
   D. Venus

5. Where does the narrator hide the old man's dismembered body in "The Tell-Tale Heart"?

    A. Under the floorboards
    B. In the attic
    C. In a dumpster
    D. Under the bed

6. What nonhuman animal appears on Montresor's coat of arms?

    A. A dog
    B. A rat
    C. A serpent
    D. A bear

7. In which country does William Wilson murder his double?

    A. Italy
    B. France
    C. Sweden
    D. England

8. In "The Murders in the Rue Morgue," what piece of evidence indicates to Dupin that the owner of the Ourang-Outang is a sailor?

    A. Flippers
    B. Naval stationery
    C. A knotted ribbon
    D. An embroidered handkerchief

9. What geographical feature forms the front yard of the Usher mansion?

    A. A flower garden
    B. High grass
    C. A mud pit
    D. A tarn

10. As what does Fortunato dress for the carnival?

    A.   A bullfighter
    B.   A black-masked villain
    C.   A court jester
    D.   A French musketeer

11. What does William Wilson wear at the duke's ball?

    A.   A Spanish cloak
    B.   A red mask
    C.   A jester's skirt
    D.   A monk's robes

12. At what time of night does the mysterious guest arrive in "The Masque of the Red Death"?

    A.   Nine
    B.   Ten
    C.   Eleven
    D.   Midnight

13. Which group of writers does the narrator of "MS. Found in a Bottle" originally dislike?

    A.   French symbolists
    B.   Italian romantics
    C.   German moralists
    D.   American realists

14. Who saves the narrator in "The Pit and the Pendulum"?

    A.   General George Washington
    B.   General Lasalle
    C.   General Patton
    D.   General Mills

15. In what city does Minister D—— from "The Purloined Letter" insult Dupin?

    A.   Paris
    B.   Vienna
    C.   Hamburg
    D.   Rome

REVIEW & RESOURCES

16. Which of the following schools does William Wilson attend?

    A. Harvard
    B. Cambridge
    C. Eton
    D. Winchester

17. With what does Fortunato indicate to Montresor that he is a Mason?

    A. A hand signal
    B. A trowel
    C. A secret slogan
    D. A piece of paper

18. In which country does the narrator of "Ligeia" purchase an abbey?

    A. America
    B. Germany
    C. France
    D. England

19. In "The Murders in the Rue Morgue," whom do the police originally arrest?

    A. The narrator
    B. Henri Cuvier
    C. Adolpe Le Bon
    D. Alexander von Humboldt

20. In "The Black Cat," what shape does the second cat's white fur form?

    A. A judge's gavel
    B. The gallows
    C. The scales of justice
    D. An electric chair

21. In "The Murders in the Rue Morgue," where does the narrator first meet Dupin?

    A. In a coffee shop
    B. At a party
    C. At a convention
    D. In a library

22. Which element of torture does the narrator encounter last in "The Pit and the Pendulum"?

    A. Hot walls
    B. A sharp pendulum
    C. Hungry rats
    D. A deep pit

23. On which night of his observation of the old man does the narrator from "The Tell-Tale Heart" commit murder?

    A. The first
    B. The eighth
    C. The seventh
    D. The third

24. The mysterious guest in "The Masque of the Red Death" comes dressed as what?

    A. A court jester
    B. A bullfighter
    C. A bloody corpse
    D. A French aristocrat

25. Along with the narrator, who survives the first hurricane in "MS. Found in a Bottle"?

    A. A young Frenchman
    B. An old Swede
    C. A bitter Italian
    D. A smart American

SUGGESTIONS FOR FURTHER READING

DAYAN, JOAN. *Fables of Mind: An Inquiry into Poe's Fiction.* New York: Oxford University Press, 1987.

ELMER, JONATHAN. *Reading at the Social Limit: Affect, Mass Culture, and Edgar Allan Poe.* Palo Alto, California: Stanford University Press, 1995.

HOFFMAN, DANIEL. *Poe, Poe, Poe, Poe, Poe, Poe, Poe.* Garden City, New York: Doubleday, 1972.

KENNEDY, J. G. *Poe, Death, and the Life of Writing.* New Haven, Connecticut: Yale University Press, 1987.

MATTHIESSEN, F. O. *American Renaissance: Art and Expression in the Age of Emerson and Whitman.* London: Oxford University Press, 1941.

PUNTER, DAVID. *The Literature of Terror: A History of Gothic Fictions from 1765 to the Present Day.* London: Longman, 1980.

QUINN, ARTHUR HOBSON. *Edgar Allan Poe: A Critical Biography.* New York: D. Appleton-Century, 1941.

ROSENHEIM, SHAWN. *The Cryptographic Imagination: Secret Writing from Edgar Poe to the Internet.* Baltimore: Johns Hopkins University Press, 1997.

SILVERMAN, KENNETH. *Edgar A. Poe: Mournful and Never-ending Remembrance.* New York: Harper Perennial, 1991.

TODOROV, TZVETAN. *The Fantastic: A Structural Approach to a Literary Genre.* Tr. Richard Howard. Ithaca, New York: Cornell University Press, 1975.

REVIEW & RESOURCES

SparkNotes
Test Preparation
Guides

The SparkNotes team figured it was time to cut standardized tests down to size. We've studied the tests for you, so that SparkNotes test prep guides are:

Smarter:
Packed with critical-thinking skills and test-
taking strategies that will improve your score.

Better:
Fully up to date, covering all new features of the tests,
with study tips on every type of question.

Faster:
Our books cover exactly what you need to
know for the test. No more, no less.

SparkNotes Study Guides: